D1155806

TITHING:
LOW-REALM,
OBSOLETE
& DEFUNCT

MATTHEW E. NARRAMORE

TEKOA PUBLISHING
GRAHAM, NORTH CAROLINA

Tithing: Low-Realm, Obsolete & Defunct
by Matthew E. Narramore

Copyright © 2004 by Matthew E. Narramore

All Rights Reserved. No part of this publication may be reproduced, stored in a retrieval system, or transmitted in any form or by any means—electronic, mechanical, digital, photocopy, recording, or any other—without prior written permission from the author, except for brief quotations in printed reviews.

Tekoa Publishing
P.O. Box 977
Graham, NC 27253

mail@tekoapublishing.com
www.tekoapublishing.com

Except where otherwise indicated, Scripture quotations in this book are taken from the King James Version of the Bible.

Cover design: Bruce DeRoos, Portland, Oregon

ISBN 0-9745587-0-2

First Edition 2004
Printed in the United States of America
12 11 10 09 08 07 06 05 04   10 9 8 7 6 5 4 3 2 1

This book is printed on acid-free paper.

*To someone who deserves a lot of credit for this book—
who insisted that it should be written and did everything she
could to see that it got finished, whose influence and inspiration
began many years before, setting an example of pursuing all
that God has made available to us through Jesus Christ
—my mother.*

CONTENTS

Even though people say that they are not preaching the Law, almost every scripture that is used to teach or promote tithing is from the Law or was speaking to people who were under the Law, not to the church.

Inadequate study of the Bible leads to the conclusion that tithing was after the Law and is still God's plan for us today. The glorious way of life that God has given the church through Jesus Christ exposes the tithing paradigm as being weak and beggarly in comparison.

The New Covenant paradigm for financial stewardship and giving is based on a completely different spiritual paradigm than the tithe and is far superior to it, just as the New Covenant in Jesus Christ is far superior to any previous relationship between God and man.

The church has been defrauded of its glorious spiritual inheritance in Christ by spiritual disinformation—wrong doctrine that destroys the power of Christ's work on the cross.

Analysis and exposé of wrong teachings such as:

▸ The tithe is the Lord's.

▸ If you don't tithe you are a God-robber.

▸ A curse will come on you if you don't tithe.

▸ We are commanded to prove God with the tithe.

designed for a different way of living than was
known before the resurrection.

In Christ, we are sons of God now. The Father's
will is to bring us to the full spiritual stature of
Jesus Christ. Tithing was ordained for people
who had a different kind of relationship to God.

Tithing is not a neutral option. It's part of a low-
realm, obsolete, and defunct religious mentality.
It hinders the church by obscuring and negating
the truth of what it means to be a son of God
through spiritual union with Jesus Christ.

Hebrews chapter 7 does not teach or support the
doctrine of tithing for the New Testament church.
It has been misunderstood and misrepresented.

PREFACE

THIS book is about much more than tithing or not tithing. It's about setting people free from a wrong, religious mindset so they can experience the reality of New Covenant life in Christ. It's about recovering a glorious spiritual inheritance that Christians have been defrauded of, exposing wrong doctrines that negate Christ's finished work on the cross. It's about living like a righteous, new-creation son of God, born again through spiritual union with Jesus Christ by his resurrection from the dead. This book is just a beginning. Tithing is just the tip of the iceberg of carnal mentalities that dominate most of Christianity.

I was taught to tithe as a child and did so for many years without question. It was never a problem to me, spiritually or financially. I thoroughly agreed with the teaching and wasn't looking for any reason to contradict it. However, after many years of seeking God and studying his word, I have come to see the doctrine of tithing, and all other financial giving as well, in a new light—the revelation of the mystery of being in Christ.

I have two objectives in writing this book. One is that Christians would wake up and realize that tithing is part of the old carnal religious way of life and put it aside to enter the New Covenant way of living. The New Testament's description for this way of living is, *in Christ*. Religious traditions that man has created are the biggest obstacle to the glorious life of God that we were created to enjoy. Tithing is one of those well-meaning-but-misguided traditions.

Another objective is to equip Christians with a solid scriptural foundation to answer the constant barrage of teaching that is promoting tithing and keeping the church in a low-realm, religious mode of living. The doctrine of tithing has been mindlessly taught and accepted for so long that some of the most outstanding Christian leaders do not recognize how it contradicts the very foundation of the gospel they are preaching.

This book may challenge some of your deepest beliefs. It may contradict your most esteemed spiritual leaders. But no brother or sister in Christ is being personally judged or attacked. I appreciate those who have given their lives in service to the Lord and his church. The Bible tells us to "esteem them very highly in love for their work's sake" (1 Thess. 5:13). However, their teachings are at all times to be examined in the light of scripture.

This book exposes the error of some very popular teachings but does not accuse those who are teaching them. No names are ever mentioned, but you may recognize some statements. There are many well-known ministers, whom I greatly respect, that I have to disagree with when it comes to the subject of tithing.

Paul the apostle said in 1 Corinthians chapter 13, "we know in part" and "we see through a glass, darkly;" therefore, we can never expect perfect doctrinal unity. However, we can pursue a better knowledge of the truth and we can extend the love of God to one another in the process. If we disagree, we can do so respectfully. Each person must walk with God in the best way they know.

I ask you to lay aside preconceived ideas and traditional thinking, and prayerfully consider the message of this book. Its purpose is to move the church toward the highest and best that God has provided in Christ. I pray that it will be the beginning of a spiritual revolution in your life.

NOTE TO THE READER

The words *covenant* and *testament* are generally synonymous in the text of the Bible. That can lead to a misunderstanding because the word testament has also been used to name the two major sections that men have designated in the Bible: Old Testament and New Testament.

The confusion arises because each section contains scriptures that relate to other covenants besides the one for which it is named. The Old Testament refers to other covenants in addition to the one that God specifically calls the Old Covenant, the covenant that he made with Israel at Mt. Sinai. The New Testament contains the scriptures pertaining to the New Covenant, which were written to believers in Jesus Christ, but it also includes the four gospels, which actually occurred during the Old Covenant. The New Covenant did not begin until Jesus shed his blood and died on the cross.

For the sake of clarity in this book, Old Testament and New Testament will be used in reference to the two sections of the Bible. Old Covenant and New Covenant will refer to those two covenants specifically.

The Bible also refers to the Old Covenant as the law of Moses or just the law. In this book the word law is capitalized when referring to the Old Covenant—the Law. When the word law is not capitalized it is referring to any other law or law in general as a principle.

This book uses the words man and son from a spiritual perspective. The term man is used in reference to mankind, anyone of the human race, male and female, regardless of age. All references to sons of God in this book include born-again women just as much as born-again men. In Christ there is neither male nor female. (Gal. 3:28) Women in Christ are sons of God, equally as men.

1

TROJAN HORSE

TITHING is not for the church. It was never intended for men and women who are born again and filled with the Holy Spirit. It is considered to be a mark of spiritual commitment, but it's not spiritual. The devil doesn't mind tithing. He welcomes anything that will take our attention away from the truth in Christ.

Tithing is an emotional subject and passionately proclaimed to be many things: an eternal law of God, a divine principle of prosperity, a matter of honor, a financial duty, an expression of gratitude, an act of obedience. Every one of those positions is held with complete sincerity, but for a born-again believer in Jesus Christ, who lives under the New Covenant, they are all sincerely wrong. The cross of Jesus Christ not only established a New Covenant, it also gave birth to a new kind of spiritual person. The new man in Christ is in a new spiritual realm and relates to God in a way that is totally different from anyone who lived before the cross. The church has failed to understand the new way of living that God initiated in Christ. Tithing is just one aspect of the failure, but it is highly emphasized and it creates a great distraction from the truth.

OLD COVENANT PARADIGM

Most of the church today is living by an Old Covenant paradigm—their spiritual perspective or theological framework for thinking and relating to God. Although they say they are not under the Old Covenant, most Christians are trying to relate to God from a perspective that is based on the Old Covenant. They take all the facts they know about Jesus and try to fit them into spiritual patterns they see in the Old Testament books of the Bible.

The church needs to make a complete paradigm shift from the Old Covenant way of thinking and living to the New Covenant way. Mixing the two doesn't work. It's like putting new wine into old wineskins. The result is a dysfunctional system of religion, which most people consider to be normal Christianity, but is not what God intended. Tithing is one way that Christians mistakenly try to express their new nature in Christ through an obsolete system of worship and financial stewardship.

Tithing is not part of the New Covenant. There are many scriptural reasons why it isn't, why it can't be, and why God's plan for New Covenant giving is far superior in every way. Tithing is not an eternal principle or mandate from God to be followed today. It has been misinterpreted to be those things because the church has failed to comprehend the new way of living that began at the resurrection.

Tithing is a carnal way of living. It's an external regulation. It doesn't originate in the new spiritual nature of a born-again believer in Jesus Christ. You don't have to be spiritual to tithe. Many people tithe who haven't been born again. Some people tithe for honorable reasons, but that doesn't make it right, and it doesn't excuse the church for teaching it. The church hinders itself and the kingdom of God on earth by perpetuating a mentality that keeps Christians carnal and immature.

LOW-REALM CHRISTIANITY

It's no surprise that most of the church lives on a low spiritual level. The New Testament has much to say about Christians being carnal, being babies, and needing to grow up spiritually. The same issues that hindered the New Testament church are still present today.

One of the main causes of low-level Christianity is that the church has followed Old Covenant patterns of living. The church has focused its attention on learning and applying principles, rather than knowing Jesus Christ, abiding in him, and expressing his life by the power of the Holy Spirit. That's why it falls so short of the biblical standard of Christianity. The church at Jerusalem, in the book of Acts, was deeply entrenched in both the Law of Moses and Old Covenant mentalities. So is the church today. The carnal religious mind is infatuated with Old Testament paradigms and is addicted to carnal ways of living based upon them.

Tithing is not a threat to the kingdom of darkness. The devil knows the church would have much more power, as well as money, if Christians were taught how to live like sons of God, who are in a spiritual union with Jesus Christ. He also knows that Christians could grow up spiritually and begin to reign in life if the confusion that comes from mixing the Old Covenant and New Covenant spiritual paradigms was removed from the church. That is more frightening to him than the increase of money that would flow into the church if the tithing mentality was abandoned.

STRATEGIC DECEPTION

From Greek legend we have the story of the Trojan War. The Greeks laid siege to the city of Troy for ten years. Failing to succeed by direct attack, they devised a brilliant strategy. Boarding their ships and sailing away, they left behind a huge wooden horse filled with soldiers. The Trojans brought the horse into their city, thinking it would give them special power. That night Greek soldiers exited the horse and attacked. Troy was conquered.

That is how Satan works against the church. He can't defeat it by direct attack so he uses deception. Power and victory come to believers through abiding in Christ with faith in his finished work. Satan's strategy is to get their attention on other things that promise results but cannot deliver. The devil's wooden horse is made of laws, rules, principles, formulas, and other ways of living, borrowed from men who were not in spiritual union with Jesus Christ. Tithing is one of those things.

Certainly there is some value in understanding biblical principles; even those who don't know God can benefit by applying them. But the church has continued to relate to God in the manner of Old Testament men, who were not born again and spiritually re-created in union with Christ. The church has exalted biblical principles to take the place of Jesus Christ because it doesn't know how to abide in Christ and live by his new nature within.

Knowledge of biblical principles has become an idol for Christians to trust in and build their lives upon, instead of building them on the person of Christ, who lives within them. The church has been taught to depend on principles. That has kept it from knowing Jesus and entering into the glorious life in him that is available here on earth.

LIFE BEYOND PRINCIPLES

Jesus didn't come to earth to give us a good life based on biblical principles. He came to give us life—his own divine, self-energizing, resurrection life and nature— through a living union with him. A way of life that is focused on laws, rules, and principles is carnal and cannot produce or experience what Jesus promised. Tithing is a carnal way of living. It cannot produce the glorious life that God provided for us in Christ.

Many Christians are satisfied to live like natural men: following laws, trying to please God, and seeking blessings. But that wasn't God's plan. He wanted to elevate us to a place of actual sonship in his family, seated at his right hand. And he did it through the cross.

The blood of Jesus was a perfect redemption, by which the Father now treats us as if we are perfect, as if we are Jesus. Jesus' resurrection was our resurrection, into an eternal destiny enthroned with him at the Father's right hand. The life within us by which we live is Jesus himself. We now live and relate to the Father identically as Jesus because we are one spirit with him.

The life that Jesus gave the church cannot be expressed in words, but it can be observed in actions. His followers lived and died to share the life they had received. Hot roads, rough seas, dirty prisons, and meager rations didn't stop them. Beatings, whippings, and stonings proved there was something in them that was greater than any obstacle they encountered.

The life that empowered the church to go and preach the gospel also compelled them to spare no resources to get the job done. Those who were not carrying the message were living to send others. Their giving was not motivated by enticements of earthly gain nor by fears of divine punishment. The followers of Jesus were sons of their Father in heaven, showing it by their actions. God was now living in man, expressing his nature through him. Laws and principles of giving were unnecessary. Love had taken over. Tithing was irrelevant. It was weak and beggarly compared to the glory of Christ in operation.

Where was the glory lost? How did we get to the place we are today? That is a long and complicated story. There were many twists and turns in the road, many tricks and traps and wiles of a deceiver. In the process many extra things were woven into the fabric of Christianity. Tithing was one of them. But Jesus Christ is working in his church to make it glorious. He is taking it to a place of maturity and authority, and the tithing mentality will have to be removed.

Many people say, "Tithing was before the Law, during the Law, and after the Law." That statement comes from taking all the references to tithing out of context, rolling them together, and creating a faulty doctrine. The following chapters will examine what the Bible actually says about tithing, some of the common misunderstandings, and God's new paradigm of giving and financial stewardship for the New Covenant.

2

Before the Law: Abraham

DURING the entire period of time before the Law there were only two Biblical references to tithing. One instance has been superficially interpreted to justify a teaching that is contrary to the New Covenant. The other is an example of unbelief and bargaining with God. Neither one can change the finished work of the cross. Neither one can add to the surpassing greatness of life in Christ. Neither one is teaching tithing to the church.

The first mention of a tithe is in Genesis 14. A group of four kings from the east came into Canaan to attack a group of five that had rebelled and quit paying tribute. Sodom was one of the cities plundered, and Abraham's nephew, Lot, was carried away with the captives. Abraham, 318 of his trained servants, and three other men of the area who were in covenant with him pursued the invaders and slaughtered them.

When Abraham returned with the people and the goods, the new king of Sodom came out to meet him. Melchizedek, king of Salem, also came out with bread and wine and pronounced a blessing upon Abraham. Genesis 14:20 says that Abraham "gave him tithes of all." Hebrews 7:4 confirms that it was a tenth of the spoils of the battle.

The king of Sodom then asked for the people to be returned to him but told Abraham to keep all the goods. By right of conquest Abraham could have kept everything, including the people. However, he refused to keep anything and publicly affirmed his oath to God that he would take nothing so that the king of Sodom could not say he had made Abraham rich.

THE FACTS VERSUS SPECULATION

The account of Abraham and Melchizedek has led people in favor of tithing to make many speculations that have no basis in scripture. An objective look at the facts leads to a different conclusion. For the sake of emphasis, the following points are listed individually.

- ▸ God's original promise to Abraham was based on nothing except faith. It had nothing to do with tithing.

- ▸ God's covenant with Abraham, which he made later to help Abraham believe, had nothing to do with tithing.

- ▸ There is no scriptural basis to say that God instructed Abraham to give a tenth of the spoils to Melchizedek.

- There is no scriptural basis to say that God ever instructed Abraham to give any tithe.

- Abraham was not made rich by giving a tithe to Melchizedek. He was already exceedingly rich before he gave it. Genesis 13 tells us that Abraham was rich in cattle, in silver and in gold. His substance was so great that the land could not bear him and Lot together. He had at least 318 male servants born in his house. The total number of persons in his company would have been much greater counting the wives and children of the servants plus others who would have stayed behind to guard his possessions.

- This is the one and only mention of Abraham giving a tithe to anyone.

- There is no scriptural basis to teach that Abraham ever gave another tithe in his entire life.

- The tithe was on the spoils of the battle.

- Abraham didn't give a tithe of his personal possessions or the increase of his flocks and herds.

- Abraham didn't give a tithe of something that he was going to keep a portion of, so it cost him nothing.

- Neither tithes nor offerings were a condition for the fulfillment of God's promise to Abraham.

- God made Abraham rich in fulfillment of his promise alone, without any kind of tithing or giving.

- There is no scriptural basis to say that Abraham's tithe to Melchizedek is God's pattern for Christians in the New Covenant.

- God's command to Abraham was to leave his country and go to the land that God would show him.

▸ God promised that he would make Abraham a great nation, he would bless him, he would make his name great, Abraham would be a blessing, he would bless them that bless Abraham, he would curse them that curse Abraham, and in Abraham all families of the earth would be blessed.

▸ Abraham believed what God said and acted on it. God considered him righteous, fulfilled his promise, and made him rich on the basis of that faith alone. Tithing had absolutely nothing to do with it.

Tithing was not part of Abraham's covenant. There is no question about that. Tithing was not the reason for his prosperity or the fulfillment of God's promises to him. Abraham was already extremely wealthy before he ever met Melchizedek. God made Abraham rich on the basis of his promise alone.

NOT AN ETERNAL PRINCIPLE

Why did Abraham give Melchizedek a tithe? Some say he was following an eternal principle. That couldn't be true because God himself gave specific instructions that were different in Numbers 31. It was another situation involving the spoils of battle. The high priest got one five-hundredth of half the spoils (one tenth of 1 percent of the total) and the Levites got one fiftieth of half the spoils (1 percent of the total). Numbers 31 is examined in more detail in chapter 4, *During the Law*.

Many people have the mistaken idea that 10 percent is a sacred standard in God's kingdom when it comes to giving. They think it was an unspoken commandment or principle that didn't get recorded until the Law was given. But that conclusion is wrong. The Bible itself clearly contradicts it. If Abraham had been following a universal principle when he gave a tenth of the spoils to Melchizedek, then God would have told the people in Numbers 31 to do the same thing. But he specifically gave them different instructions—proof that Abraham wasn't following an eternal law and his tithe isn't a pattern to be followed today.

There was no commandment before the Law that man should tithe. There is no scriptural basis to say that tithing was an unspoken commandment or a universal principle of worship. There is no scriptural proof that any other worshipper of the true God ever gave anyone a tithe during that time, including Jacob. There is no scriptural basis to say that God wanted a tithe from anyone during that time. Those are the facts. Anything else is speculation.

There is much debate about the identity of Melchizedek. There are at least four schools of thought among Bible scholars and leaders in the church and each position has its scriptural arguments. However, when it comes to the question of tithing in the life of a Christian today, it absolutely doesn't matter who Melchizedek was or why he was given a tithe by Abraham. The key to the matter is profoundly simple, but many in the church have missed it.

THE REAL ISSUE

Those who argue about Abraham and Melchizedek are missing the real issue of life in the New Covenant. We are not Abraham and we are not living before the Law. The death and resurrection of Jesus Christ is the focal point of history. It changed the entire nature of man's relationship to God. No matter who Melchizedek was or why Abraham gave him a tithe, it doesn't change the truth or spirit of the New Covenant. Tithing is not part of the New Covenant. Tithing detracts from it. Financial stewardship in the New Covenant is based on a different paradigm.

We do know that Melchizedek was a king and a priest and that Abraham gave him a tithe of the spoils. Tithers argue that Jesus is both king and priest and is therefore due a tithe. Jesus is certainly worthy of a tithe and much more, but his kingdom and priesthood are not based on the tithe. The tithe has no place in it. Everything about tithing is inferior to New Covenant life in Christ.

Jesus never called anyone to a ten-percent commitment. His call was to absolute abandonment of all things for him and absolute commitment of all things to him. He never sanctioned the tithe as a standard of giving in his new kingdom that would begin with his resurrection. He required his followers to forsake all, to give all, and to use all for the accomplishment of his purposes. Paradoxically, he entrusts all things to his disciples to jointly possess with him and use in his service. And the Holy Spirit is now the leader in all matters, not the tithe principle.

The story of Melchizedek was later used by the Holy Spirit as a prophetic picture to the nation of Israel about a new covenant and spiritual order that would replace the Law of Moses. Psalm 110 spoke prophetically about the Messiah and said he would be a priest forever after the order of Melchizedek. Under the Old Covenant, the office of the king was separate from the office of the priest. The resurrected Lord Jesus Christ is both king and priest, and that is one way in which he fulfills the prophetic pattern of being a priest after the order of Melchizedek.

Hebrews 7 compares the priesthood of Melchizedek and the Levitical priesthood but leaves much of the mystery unrevealed. The writer of Hebrews himself said that there was much more that he couldn't say because the people he was writing to were dull of hearing. However, when it comes to the question of tithing, Paul's writings about life in Christ make it so clear that tithing is not part of the New Covenant that we don't need to solve the mystery of Melchizedek in order to know what we should do today.

SCRIPTURAL CONCLUSIONS

Having the benefit of the rest of the Bible to help us know and understand God, we can see beneath the surface of Abraham's situation to make some conclusions that agree with the truth that God revealed in Christ.

- ▸ Abraham was righteous by faith alone.

- ▸ God was glorified in blessing Abraham and making him rich by grace alone.

- ▸ Abraham's prosperity was not based on tithing or financial giving.

- ▸ Abraham's faith led to his prosperity. He believed God's word and acted on it. He left family and home and followed God, not knowing where he was going.

▶ God values and rewards faith above all else. He responds with grace beyond natural comprehension.

▶ The most important things in God's kingdom are clearly revealed. Anything as important as an eternal, universal law of tithing would have been clearly communicated. It would not have been left to speculation and presumption.

▶ Ten percent is not an eternally sacred standard of giving. God required much more than the tithe under the Law of Moses. There were many more sacrifices and offerings that were commanded. Many interpret the Law to require two separate tithes and some believe that it required three.

▶ The implicit condition of God's covenant with Abraham was that everything God had was committed to Abraham and everything Abraham had was committed to God, and each must be willing at all times to use all their resources for the benefit of the other. In that kind of relationship tithing becomes immaterial. It is surpassed by the greater commitment of using 100 percent for the accomplishment of God's purposes.

▶ Tithing is immaterial in the New Covenant also. God is seeking mature sons who will walk with him on the level of total commitment.

ISAAC AND THE COVENANT

The next significant figure in the covenant lineage after Abraham was his son Isaac. Was tithing part of his covenant with God? Was it the source of his wealth? What was his responsibility toward God in regard to his wealth? How does his story apply to us in the New Covenant?

Isaac was very wealthy from inheriting all his father's possessions. When famine came into the land the Lord appeared to him and reconfirmed the promise made to Abraham. God told Isaac not to go down to Egypt but to dwell where he would tell him and that he would be with him and bless him. Those were the only instructions that Isaac received from God. Isaac obeyed and God blessed him. Genesis 26:13–14 says:

> And the man waxed great, and went forward, and grew until he became very great: For he had possession of flocks, and possession of herds, and great store of servants: and the Philistines envied him.

God did not command Isaac to make sacrifices or to tithe. The Bible tells us that Isaac built an altar and called upon the name of the Lord, but that was voluntary just like the altars his father, Abraham, built. There is no scriptural basis to say that Isaac ever gave a tithe of anything to anyone in his entire life. There is no indication that there was ever any concept of a tithe included in his relationship to God. Isaac obeyed the instructions that God gave to him personally, to sojourn in the land instead of going to Egypt. He did that by faith and God protected him and increased the great wealth he already had.

Of course, the nature of the covenant that Isaac had with God was that he and all his possessions were completely dedicated to God. He had to live his entire life with the understanding that at any time and for any reason God could make a demand on anything he possessed. That is how his father, Abraham, had to live also. When Abraham was commanded to offer Isaac as a sacrifice, he had to prove his faith and his commitment to the covenant.

That is the nature of covenant, one-hundred-percent commitment from both parties. That is the nature of our relationship to God through Christ. And like Isaac, we don't concern ourselves with commandments that we have not been given. We need to consider what one-hundred-percent commitment means to us personally in our own calling. We need to listen for God's specific instruction, direction, and requirement for us personally.

The only other mention of a tithe before the Law is in the life of Isaac's son Jacob. A thoughtful study of the situation reveals that it is not what it has been made to be. It does not support the practice of tithing in the New Covenant. In fact, it is the record of a person with no faith who was trying to manipulate God. Jacob did the opposite of what would have honored and pleased God.

3

BEFORE THE LAW: JACOB

THE story of Jacob's promise to give God a tithe begins on his journey to Haran, the home of his mother's family. (Gen. 28) Jacob had gotten the birthright that belonged to his brother, Esau, by taking advantage of a weak moment. Then by deception he had stolen the special blessing reserved for the firstborn as well. So, in addition to the greater inheritance and privileges that belonged to the firstborn, Jacob also had an extra blessing that would further empower him to prosper.

Esau was furious and was planning to murder Jacob for revenge. Jacob had to flee for safety, but before he left, his father, Isaac, spoke a final blessing upon him and his seed, to receive the blessing of Abraham and to inherit the land that God had given him. At this point in time Jacob has been extremely blessed. He has the family birthright, the family blessing, and the blessing of Abraham conferred upon him as well. He should have a strong sense of blessing and confidence in his life but he doesn't, as we shall see by his actions.

On his journey to Haran, Jacob spent a night at a place he named Bethel. As he slept he dreamed and saw the Lord standing at the top of a ladder that went from earth to heaven. In Genesis 28:13–15 we have the account of what the Lord said to him.

> And, behold, the LORD stood above it, and said, I am the LORD God of Abraham thy father, and the God of Isaac: the land whereon thou liest, to thee will I give it, and to thy seed;

> And thy seed shall be as the dust of the earth, and thou shalt spread abroad to the west, and to the east, and to the north, and to the south: and in thee and in thy seed shall all the families of the earth be blessed.

> And, behold, I am with thee, and will keep thee in all places whither thou goest, and will bring thee again into this land; for I will not leave thee, until I have done that which I have spoken to thee of.

God told Jacob what he was going to do for him: give the land to him and his seed, multiply his seed, be with him and protect him wherever he went, and bring him back home again. It was God's promise to him and it was based on faith alone. It did not depend on any conditional requirements such as tithes, offerings, or sacrifices. It was based on the original promise to Abraham which was based on faith alone without any tithes, offerings, or sacrifices either. All God wanted Jacob to do was to believe him. God wanted to keep the promise for Jacob just like he did for Abraham, who became the father of faith.

When Abraham had trouble believing God's original promise, God confirmed it to him by a covenant. But even then God put Abraham into a deep sleep and walked through the slain animals without him. There was no contribution made by Abraham that obligated God to make the covenant or to fulfill it. Abraham is known for his faith. That was his part in his relationship with God.

In God's covenant with Abraham, Isaac, and Jacob there is absolutely no sense of any tithe, offering, or sacrifice made by the men to gain the benefits and blessings they received. God came to them and made promises that covered every area of their lives and required nothing from them but faith. Abraham was eventually required to prove his willingness to offer his son as a sacrifice. That in effect was a test of his faith because everything God had promised him was depending on Isaac.

JACOB'S UNBELIEF

Jacob didn't respond to God's promise in the same way that his father and grandfather did. Abraham and Isaac accepted the promise by faith and continued on with their lives as God directed, but not Jacob. In Genesis 28:16–22 we see how he responded:

And Jacob awaked out of his sleep, and he said, Surely the LORD is in this place; and I knew it not.

And he was afraid, and said, How dreadful is this place! this is none other but the house of God, and this is the gate of heaven.

And Jacob rose up early in the morning, and took the stone that he had put for his pillows, and set it up for a pillar, and poured oil upon the top of it.

And he called the name of that place Bethel: but the name of that city was called Luz at the first.

And Jacob vowed a vow, saying, If God will be with me, and will keep me in this way that I go, and will give me bread to eat, and raiment to put on,

So that I come again to my father's house in peace; then shall the LORD be my God:

And this stone, which I have set for a pillar, shall be God's house: and of all that thou shalt give me I will surely give the tenth unto thee.

Faith takes God at his word; Jacob did not. Jacob responded to God's promise by making a vow, which showed his unbelief. He said, "if" you will do all this "then" you will be my God and I will give you a tenth of everything you give me. God had just promised to bless, protect, and fulfill the original promise that he made to Abraham. He didn't ask for a tithe or anything else. Jacob ignored what God had just promised and started trying to manipulate him by making a vow. His vow was a deal he was making with God. He had more faith in a foolish bargain than he did in God's word.

Jacob had more evidence to base his faith upon than Abraham and Isaac had when God came to them. Jacob had the benefit of hearing all the stories of what God had done in their lives. He had grown up in the great wealth that God had blessed them with. But when God made the same promise to Jacob that he had made to his father and grandfather, he didn't respond in faith like they did. Abraham left his country to go to an unknown destination. Jacob wouldn't even commit to having the Lord as his God.

FAITH PLEASES GOD

God didn't ask for a tithe. He wanted faith. Besides, God expected more than a tithe; he expected one-hundred-percent commitment. This is a lesson that Jacob was very slow to learn. It wasn't until returning about twenty years later, when he wrestled with God all night at the brook Jabbok, that he finally committed himself to God.

God would have preferred a response of faith instead of the promise of a tithe, which was just a bargain based on fear and unbelief. The same is true today. God is looking for faith but many people are tithing out of fear. They are afraid their needs will not be met if they quit tithing. Fear-based giving does not please God and neither does the preaching that promotes it. "For whatsoever is not of faith is sin." (Rom. 14:23b)

During the period of time before the Law, God purposely made the issue of sacrifices and offerings to be a matter of freewill so that they could be a true expression of faith and worship. God prefers not to cheapen his relationship with man by setting requirements for offerings.

Concerning Jacob's vow to give God a tenth, we don't know what he had in mind. Did he plan to sacrifice a tenth of his wealth on an altar? That isn't the usual concept of a tithe—normally given to someone for their use, not for sacrificial destruction. Did he think he would find a priest and give him a tenth? It's not likely that there were any other worshippers of the true God in the entire land of Canaan other than the descendants of Abraham. Even if there were, God had not yet ordained any formal system of worship that included giving and receiving tithes.

God didn't institute a priesthood or a system of tithing to support them until the Law of Moses was given. Unless Melchizedek was actually a pre-incarnate appearance of Jesus Christ it isn't likely that he was still alive when Jacob returned from Haran. According to estimates of biblical dates, Jacob's return from Haran was about 170 years after the time Abraham met Melchizedek.

God didn't praise Jacob for his vow to give him a tenth. The Bible doesn't even say if Jacob ever paid it. Apparently it was not an important thing in God's sight. After all, it wasn't God's idea. It wasn't an act of faith. It was just faithless deal-making by a man who really didn't know God.

God had kept his word to Abraham and Isaac without any vows on their part. He had blessed, protected, and made them rich according to his promise alone. Maybe when Jacob wrestled all night with God at the river Jabbok he realized that God had never wanted a tithe, he only wanted faith.

UNDERSTANDING SCRIPTURE

Just because a story is in the Bible doesn't mean that it portrays the will of God for the people involved. It certainly doesn't mean that it is God's will for us today in the New Covenant. The Bible records many things that men did which were not the will of God.

In the book of Judges, chapter 11, we have the story of Jephthah, a man used by God as a deliverer for the nation of Israel. In verse 29 we read that the Spirit of the Lord came upon him. Therefore, we know that God was with him and he was anointed to do battle and be victorious over the enemy he was about to face. However, Jephthah didn't feel confident to trust God alone, so he made a vow in an attempt to make a deal with God that would guarantee his success.

> And Jephthah vowed a vow unto the LORD, and said, If thou shalt without fail deliver the children of Ammon into mine hands,
>
> Then it shall be, that whatsoever cometh forth of the doors of my house to meet me, when I return in peace from the children of Ammon, shall surely be the LORD'S, and I will offer it up for a burnt offering. (Judg. 11:30–31)

Jephthah went out to battle and the Lord gave him victory, but when he returned he had the grief of keeping the vow he made.

> And Jephthah came to Mizpeh unto his house, and, behold, his daughter came out to meet him with timbrels and with dances: and she was his only child; beside her he had neither son nor daughter.

> And it came to pass, when he saw her, that he rent his clothes, and said, Alas, my daughter! thou hast brought me very low, and thou art one of them that trouble me: for I have opened my mouth unto the LORD, and I cannot go back. (Judg. 11:34–35)

Jephthah gave his daughter two months to go and mourn with her friends in the mountains of Israel. The Bible then records the tragic ending of Jephthah's sincere-but-misguided theology.

> And it came to pass at the end of two months, that she returned unto her father, who did with her according to his vow which he had vowed: (Judg. 11:39a)

The Old Testament and the New Testament both record many things people did out of ignorance that were not the will or plan of God. Their stories are included for our benefit but they are not all patterns for us to follow today. We have to rightly divide the scripture to apply it to our lives correctly. Life in the New Covenant is based on spiritual union with Jesus Christ, not on past examples of people who weren't born again. The resurrected Lord Jesus Christ is the model for us today.

Scriptural Conclusions

Therefore, in regard to the statement that tithing was before the Law:

- ▸ There is no scriptural record of any commandment, instruction, or suggestion by God related to a tithe prior to the Law of Moses.

- ▸ During the entire period of time before the Law there are only two biblical references to a tithe and in neither case is there any indication that the people were instructed by God to do what they did.

- ▸ The tithe that Abraham gave to Melchizedek was not explained or given much attention.

- ▸ The tithe proposed by Jacob was an example of doubt and unbelief. We have no details about how he planned to pay it and no record that he ever did.

- ▸ God did not require certain amounts for sacrifices and offerings because that would destroy the nature of the offering and would ruin what God was looking for in his relationship with man.

- ▸ In regard to the question of whether Christians should tithe today, it doesn't matter what Abraham or Jacob did before the Law. We have a relationship to God through Jesus Christ that is completely different than Abraham's relationship to Melchizedek. It is far higher and better than anything that Abraham or Jacob could have imagined. There is no reason or advantage to us or the kingdom of God to go back and pick up an obsolete spiritual paradigm.

The next period of time to be considered is during the
Law. The scriptural references to tithing during this period
are also misinterpreted and wrongly applied to the church.
An objective study of tithing during the Law reveals some
important facts.

4

DURING THE LAW

DURING the Law, tithing was part of God's system to provide for the priests, the Levites, and the poor in Israel. But it was only one part of God's financial program under the Law. There were many other gifts, sacrifices, offerings, and financially oriented commandments that were included in that system. The general perception of tithing during the Law is simplistic and inaccurate. That misunderstanding contributes to the wrong conclusion that Christians should tithe today.

Tithing under the Law was not just a simple 10 percent. There were many more details. Many people interpret the Law to mean that there were two separate tithes required. Some believe that there were actually three. There were also special instructions for the administration of the tithe based on a cyclical pattern. There was a three-year cycle, a seven-year cycle and a fifty-year cycle.

Tithing under the Law was not a blanket 10 percent from any and every source of financial increase. Law by its nature is specific. The Law specifically defined the "tithe" and the process of "tithing." It was to come from the land. It was the increase of fields, vineyards, trees, flocks, herds, and honey from beehives. (Lev. 27:30, 32; Deut. 12:17, 14:22, 23; 2 Chron. 31:5, 6; Neh. 10:37, 12:44, 13:5, 12)

NOT A UNIVERSAL PRINCIPLE

The scripture is clear that tithing wasn't a universal principle during the Law. The "tithe" was a tenth of the designated things and nothing else. The wide variety of other business activities and sources of financial gain that were part of the economy, such as labor, skilled trades, professional services, commercial enterprise, rents, and inheritance were not included. If God wanted to include them he would have named them specifically or representatively or he would have clearly said that every source was included. When God means any, every, or all, he says so. The Law allowed for freewill offerings from other sources but they were not the "tithe" and were not called the "tithe."

Spoils of battle were not included in the law of tithing either. In Numbers 31 the children of Israel fought the Midianites, and the Lord gave Moses special instructions about the spoils that were taken. If tithing was an eternal, universal principal in God's kingdom then no special instructions would have been needed. Instead, the people would have simply been told to bring a tenth. But God told them to do something very different. There were four categories which were to be divided a certain way: sheep, cattle, donkeys, and virgin women. The spoils of gold and jewelry were not included in the mandatory offerings.

All of the spoils in the first four categories were divided in half. Half went to the men who fought in the battle, and half was given to the rest of the congregation. Out of the half that belonged to the men of war, one five-hundredth was given to Eleazar the priest for a heave offering of the Lord. Out of the half that belonged to the congregation, one fiftieth was given to the Levites. So the high priest got one tenth of 1 percent of the total spoils and the Levites got 1 percent of the total spoils. These were specific instructions from the Lord and they had nothing to do with the tithe or 10 percent.

The men who fought in the battle were thankful that not one Israelite man had lost his life; so they also brought a voluntary oblation to the Lord of the jewels, gold, chains, bracelets, rings, earrings, and ornaments. There was no set percentage or amount. Out of all the required and voluntary offerings from the spoils of this battle, none of it was included in the law pertaining to tithing. This passage of scripture is an extra confirmation that tithing is not a universal principle in God's kingdom, and that Abraham was not following some unwritten universal principle when he gave a tenth of the spoils to Melchizedek.

Firstfruits was another kind of offering under the Law. It was a different offering than the tithe, based on a different concept. Many people use the word firstfruits incorrectly, as if it were synonymous with tithing. That is a source of much confusion and wrong teaching. People know that God should always be first. So because they confuse firstfruits with the tithe, they believe that tithing is the eternal principle for putting God first.

PUTTING GOD FIRST IS INFERIOR

Actually, putting God first is a misunderstanding in itself. If something is first it means that something else is second, and whatever is first is just one of many others. In the New Covenant, God is first, last, and everything in between. He is the only thing. He is the all in all. There is nothing else. In Christ everything is dedicated to God and everything is used for his eternal purpose. The notion of putting God first is inferior to the New Covenant man; Christ is everything to him and everything he does is in Christ. Anything less than that has no place.

When people try to put God first they end up with a lot of rules and principles for how that should be done. If they would let God be what he wants to be, the source of everything in their life, they would be free to follow the leading of the Holy Spirit without regard to any rules on how to put him first or how to be a good Christian.

The Law was an indivisible unit. It was a comprehensive set of instructions to regulate the nation of Israel on every level: personal, family, community, and national. A common error in the church is to believe that certain parts of the Law passed away, but that other parts still pertain to us. The New Testament scriptures make it plain that if you put yourself under any part of the Law then you are under the whole Law.

> For whosoever shall keep the whole law, and yet offend in one point, he is guilty of all. (James 2:10)

> For I testify again to every man that is circumcised, that he is a debtor to do the whole law. (Gal. 5:3)

Tithing during the Law has nothing to do with life in the New Covenant. All of the commandments, instructions, rebukes, exhortations, blessings, and curses related to tithing during the Law were for the people who were under the Law. They are not for the church. It is wrong to take scriptures that were given to Israel while they were living under the Law of Moses and use them to teach tithing to Christians. It brings spiritual confusion and weakness into the church. That is what is being done every time someone reads Malachi 3:10, "Bring ye all the tithes into the storehouse…," or declares "the tithe is the Lord's" (Lev. 27:30) for the purpose of compelling people to tithe. Tithing is one of the church's self-contradicting doctrines that are based on scriptures that are taken out of context.

GIFTS ARE VOLUNTARY

During the Law there was a difference between freewill offerings and those that were required. The tithe, which was required, was not really a gift. It was a tax. Freewill gifts were voluntary expressions of love for God that came from the heart.

> And when ye will offer a sacrifice of thanksgiving
> unto the LORD, offer it at your own will. (Lev.
> 22:29)

In Exodus we have the account of a freewill offering that was received for the purpose of constructing the tabernacle and all its furnishings. It was completely voluntary.

> Speak unto the children of Israel, that they bring
> me an offering: of every man that giveth it will-
> ingly with his heart ye shall take my offering.
> (Exod. 25:2)

> And Moses spake unto all the congregation of the
> children of Israel, saying, This is the thing which
> the LORD commanded, saying,

> Take ye from among you an offering unto the
> LORD: whosoever is of a willing heart, let him
> bring it... (Exod. 35:4,5a)

In Exodus 35:21–29 the people began to bring their offering, and we can sense the joy of the occasion.

> And they came, every one whose heart stirred him
> up, and every one whom his spirit made willing,
> and they brought the LORD'S offering to the work
> of the tabernacle of the congregation, and for all his
> service, and for the holy garments.

> And they came, both men and women, as many as
> were willing hearted, and brought bracelets, and
> earrings, and rings, and tablets, all jewels of gold:

and every man that offered offered an offering of gold unto the LORD.

And every man, with whom was found blue, and purple, and scarlet, and fine linen, and goats' hair, and red skins of rams, and badgers' skins, brought them.

Every one that did offer an offering of silver and brass brought the LORD'S offering: and every man, with whom was found shittim wood for any work of the service, brought it.

And all the women that were wise hearted did spin with their hands, and brought that which they had spun, both of blue, and of purple, and of scarlet, and of fine linen.

And all the women whose heart stirred them up in wisdom spun goats' hair.

And the rulers brought onyx stones, and stones to be set, for the ephod, and for the breastplate;

And spice, and oil for the light, and for the anointing oil, and for the sweet incense.

The children of Israel brought a willing offering unto the LORD, every man and woman, whose heart made them willing to bring for all manner of work, which the LORD had commanded to be made by the hand of Moses.

The giving continued as the people brought more and more every morning.

> And they brought yet unto him free offerings every morning. (Exod. 36:3b)

Finally there was too much and the people had to be stopped.

> And they spake unto Moses, saying, The people bring much more than enough for the service of the work, which the LORD commanded to make.
>
> And Moses gave commandment, and they caused it to be proclaimed throughout the camp, saying, Let neither man nor woman make any more work for the offering of the sanctuary. So the people were restrained from bringing.
>
> For the stuff they had was sufficient for all the work to make it, and too much. (Exod. 36:5–7)

That was the grace of God in operation. It was a preview of the age that we are now living in and how much better it is. Grace always outperforms law, every time, every way. The focus of the church on tithing is counterproductive. Neither the threats nor the promises that go with the message of tithing can motivate people to give as much as love in a heart that is overwhelmed by grace.

The church longs for the day when people will have to be told to stop giving, the day when there will be more than enough to meet every need. That day will come when the tithing mentality is gone and pure grace reigns in the hearts and minds of believers. Christians will open their hearts and hold nothing back from God's service when they see the truth of what God has done for them in Christ by grace alone.

Tithing is a tradition that causes people to read the Bible with a bias and come to wrong conclusions. Many who say tithing was "after the Law" don't realize when the Law ended and when the New Covenant began. Some of the scriptures that they think were after the Law were actually during the Law. There is one reference to tithing that is truly after the Law, but it is part of a larger argument in the book of Hebrews that has been carelessly read, wrongly interpreted, and misapplied. It is not teaching tithing to the New Testament church.

5

AFTER THE LAW

THE statement that tithing was "after the Law" is not true. Part of the error comes from not considering when the Old Covenant ended and when the New Covenant began. When Jesus referred to tithing, the Law was still in effect. It didn't end until he died on the cross. Jesus was living during the Law and speaking to people who were under the Law.

Jesus mentioned tithing three times in the New Testament. In Matthew 23:23 and Luke 11:42, Jesus acknowledged to the Pharisees that they tithed and should do so. He described how they tithed the minute quantities of their herbs, but he rebuked them for omitting the weightier matters of the Law, such as judgement, mercy, and faith. He wasn't teaching the importance of tithing. He was condemning their moral corruption and the fact that they took self-righteous pride in their tithing.

There is only one other record of Jesus mentioning the tithe. In Luke 18:9–14 he told a parable about a Pharisee who gave tithes. Again, he was rebuking the Pharisees for the pride they took in their religious activities. This statement from Jesus actually foreshadows the fact that tithing would not be part of the New Covenant because the other man in the story was justified by God without tithing.

The statements Jesus made on tithing were not instructions to the church for life in the New Covenant. His death, burial, and resurrection did a radical work in the spirit realm that forever changed the way that man relates to God. Although his statements on tithing are recorded in the section of the Bible that we call the New Testament, they really occurred during the Law and pertained to that period of time.

HEBREWS CHAPTER 7

Another mistake that causes people to think that tithing was "after the Law" is a misunderstanding of Hebrews chapter 7, which is the only reference to tithing that is truly "after the Law." That passage of scripture has nothing to do with tithing in the New Covenant. Tithing is only mentioned as part of a comparison between Melchizedek and the Levitical priesthood.

The book of Hebrews proclaims the superiority of the New Covenant. It says we have a better hope, better covenant, better promises, better sacrifices, better substance, better country, better resurrection, and better outcome of our faith. It shows that Jesus has a better name and better blood, and that we now have a better cleansing of sin, a better conscience, and a better relationship with God, entering the true holy place in the heavenly realm.

Hebrews chapter 7 is arguing that Jesus is a greater priest than any priest in the Old Covenant. To make his point, the writer is first proving that Melchizedek was a greater priest than any priest in the Old Covenant. That will prove that Jesus is also greater because Psalm 110 had prophesied that Jesus would be a high priest after the order of Melchizedek.

The writer of Hebrews bases his argument on the fact that Abraham gave Melchizedek a tithe. How does that tithe make Melchizedek greater than all the Old Covenant priests? Hebrews 7 uses the following logic.

- When Abraham gave the tithe to Melchizedek, all of Abraham's unborn descendants were symbolically in his loins;

- which means that the tribe of Levi and all the Old Covenant priests were in his loins;

- which means that all the Old Covenant priests were there paying that tithe to Melchizedek;

- which means that when Abraham received the blessing from Melchizedek, all the Old Covenant priests were also there receiving the blessing from Melchizedek;

- therefore, because the one who receives the tithe and gives the blessing is greater than the one who gives the tithe and receives the blessing, Melchizedek is greater than the Old Covenant priests.

- And because Melchizedek is proven to be greater than the Old Covenant priests, that proves Jesus is also greater because he is a high priest after the order of Melchizedek.

In Hebrews 8:1 the writer sums up what has been said:

Now of the things which we have spoken this is the sum: We have such an high priest, who is set on the right hand of the throne of the Majesty in the heavens;

This verse clarifies the writer's purpose for bringing up the subject of Abraham and Melchizedek—to show that we have a greater high priest. He wasn't teaching tithing to the church either directly or indirectly.

HIGHER SPIRITUAL PARADIGM

It is true that Jesus is a great high priest forever after the order of Melchizedek and that Melchizedek received a tithe from Abraham. However, we have a completely different and much higher relationship to Jesus Christ than Abraham had to Melchizedek. It calls for a totally different way of life than that which was appropriate for Abraham.

The tithe that Abraham gave to Melchizedek is also different than the tithe that is taught in church today. It was not the basis of his financial blessing. It was given after Abraham was already exceedingly rich. It was not the basis of getting answers to any of his prayers. It was not a required or suggested part of his covenant with God. It was not something he had to do to avoid a curse. It was a tithe on something that he was not even going to keep. There is no scriptural basis to say that it was more than a one-time event in his life.

Why do Christians fight to pattern their relationship to God after the example of a man who would have given anything to trade places? New Covenant giving is based on a different spiritual paradigm than what we see in the life of Abraham. Consider Abraham's relationship with God compared to our relationship with God through Christ:

- ► Abraham had not been redeemed by the blood of Jesus.[1]

- ► Abraham's sins were not remitted (totally forgiven and washed away) they were only temporarily covered and overlooked.[2]

- ► Abraham had not been baptized into Christ by the Holy Spirit.[3]

- ► Abraham was not in an actual spiritual union with God.[4]

- ► Abraham's old nature had not been crucified with Christ.[5]

- ► Abraham had not been born again and spiritually re-created with God's own divine nature in him.[6]

- ► Abraham was not a son of God with the same standing as Jesus Christ in God's family.[7]

- ► Abraham had not been made the righteousness of God. (His faith was only counted for righteousness.)[8]

- ▸ Abraham could not say, "It is Christ that lives in me."[9]

- ▸ Abraham was not the temple of God. God did not dwell in him.[10]

- ▸ Abraham did not have the indwelling Holy Spirit to lead him.[11]

- ▸ Abraham had not been delivered out of the power of darkness and translated into the kingdom of God's Son.[12]

- ▸ Abraham had not been made alive with Christ, raised up with him, and seated with him at the Father's right hand.[13]

- ▸ Abraham had not been blessed with every spiritual blessing in heavenly places in Christ.[14]

- ▸ Abraham was not a joint owner of all things through spiritual union with the resurrected Christ.[15]

- ▸ Abraham did not have access to all authority in heaven and earth through the name of Jesus.[16]

- ▸ Abraham could not do the same works as Jesus and even greater works that Jesus said we would do, nor could he grow up into full stature in Christ.[17]

Christians who fight to follow the principle of tithing haven't seen the reality of living in Christ as a son of God. When they see the new and higher way of life in Christ they will leave the old inferior ways behind. We can learn some things from Abraham about faith, but the resurrected Lord Jesus Christ is the only true model for living and relating to God for a born-again Christian. Paul said in 1 Corinthians 11:1, "Be ye followers of me, even as I also am of Christ." Paul was following the resurrected Christ, not the Christ before the cross who was living under the Old Covenant and fulfilling the obligations of the Law.

TOTAL CHANGE OF PARADIGM

Some believe that the absence of teaching on tithing in the book of Acts and the epistles shows that it was so universally accepted it didn't need to be mentioned. That conclusion misses the real issue. The New Covenant is a total change in the way man relates to God. The change in relationship is the reason why tithing isn't mentioned. It doesn't need to be mentioned. It's a nonissue. It's irrelevant. The church has largely missed the meaning of the New Covenant.

In Acts chapter 15 we find the church in Jerusalem disputing about how the Law should pertain to the new gentile believers. This was about twenty years after the resurrection and the Jewish believers in Jerusalem were still deeply entrenched in an Old Covenant mentality. After much deliberation, James finally spoke up and said that the gentiles should not be troubled with all the aspects of the Law that the Jewish believers still kept.

The leaders in Jerusalem concluded that they would give the gentile believers only four instructions: abstain from eating food offered to idols, from eating blood, from eating anything strangled, and from fornication. This was the sum total of their instructions to the gentiles. But even some of these instructions were based on faulty theology. Paul made it clear in 1 Corinthians chapters 6, 8, and 10 that eating food offered to idols is not an issue if you have a revelation of the truth in Christ.

If tithing was as important as it is said to be, the church leaders in Jerusalem would have certainly mentioned it. This was their perfect opportunity to communicate the most important truths of the New Covenant to all the gentile believers. But even though the church in Jerusalem was hung up on the Law, only beginning to realize that a gentile did not need to convert to Judaism first before they could become a disciple of Jesus Christ, tithing was still not part of their instructions to the new gentile believers.

The church in Jerusalem exempted the gentiles from keeping the Law, but failed to realize they didn't need to keep it either. Their faith in Jesus was mixed up with an obsolete mentality about the Law, so they created a modified set of laws for the gentiles to live by. The carnal mind cannot comprehend the New Covenant. Only the Holy Spirit can reveal it. The new relationship to God through Christ operates differently than everything before it. Laws, rules, principles, regulations, guidelines, formulas, methods, and systems do not define the New Covenant. There is only one issue, that is Christ himself living within.

Christians are free to tithe because they are free to give as they purpose in their heart, but tithing has no special recognition or benefit in the New Covenant. Why go backward and seek after the kind of spiritual life that Abraham had? Why not pursue what is available to us in Christ today? The issues now are faith and following the leading of the Holy Spirit, not tithing. The very life that Christ now has is available to those who will enter into that dimension of life with him. But to do so we must leave behind the old, carnal ways of religious tradition.

It cannot be overemphasized that the key to life for a Christian is an understanding of what it means to be in Christ. Most of the church has not been taught that. Some who think they understand that truth are unknowingly negating it with other teachings and practices. Tithing is one of those practices that distracts people's attention and keeps them from the fullness of life in Christ.

The New Testament has much to say about giving that is not based on tithing. Those other teachings are often overlooked because tithing has been adopted as the foundational truth on the subject. In many cases the whole spirit of giving has been distorted and what is being taught is much different than what we see in the lives of Jesus and the apostles.

6

New Covenant Giving

THE New Covenant has a higher financial commitment than the tithe, but it's based on a completely different paradigm. Tithing is never mentioned as an instruction to New Covenant believers—not as a law, a principle, or a voluntary practice. The apostles exhorted believers to give financially, but it had nothing to do with tithing. When they instructed believers to assist the poor, the widows, and the fatherless and to support the ministers of the gospel, they never quoted scriptures about tithing.

Paul wrote more on the subject of financial giving than the other writers of New Testament epistles. When he instructed believers about their obligations to give financially he quoted Old Testament scriptures to support his teaching, but not the ones about tithing. There is no basis to say the New Testament church considered tithing to be the pattern for financial stewardship. There is no scriptural evidence to say the apostles considered tithing to be an eternal principle for all ages or the key to financial blessing for Christians.

In 1 Corinthians 9, Paul presents an extensive teaching on why ministers of the gospel have a right to be supported financially and why the body of Christ is obligated to do so. He appeals to several theological arguments to prove what he is teaching. This would be the perfect opportunity for him to quote a verse on tithing as the scriptural authority for what he is saying but he doesn't.

In 1 Corinthians 9:7 he begins his instruction by appealing to common sense.

> Who goeth a warfare any time at his own charges? who planteth a vineyard, and eateth not of the fruit thereof? or who feedeth a flock, and eateth not of the milk of the flock?

In verse nine he refers to the Law of Moses which says: "Thou shalt not muzzle the ox when he treadeth out the corn." (Deut. 25:4)

In verse thirteen of 1 Corinthians 9, Paul refers to the Old Testament principle that those who serve in the temple and at the altar are ordained to partake of those things that are brought as sacrifices and offerings. In verse fourteen he quotes the words of Jesus:

> Even so hath the Lord ordained that they which preach the gospel should live of the gospel.

This is a reference to what Jesus told the disciples when he sent them out. (Matt. 10:10, "...for the workman is worthy of his meat," and Luke 10:7, "...for the labourer is worthy of his hire.")

In 1 Timothy 5, Paul teaches believers to support the ministers of the gospel. He again quotes Deuteronomy 25:4 and the words of Jesus but he says nothing about tithing.

> Let the elders that rule well be counted worthy of double honour, especially they who labour in the word and doctrine. For the scripture saith, Thou shalt not muzzle the ox that treadeth out the corn. And, The labourer is worthy of his reward. (1 Tim. 5:17–18)

Jesus also said many things on the subject of giving that were not based on tithing. A thorough study of all the New Testament exhortations that apply to financial giving reveals a different perspective than what is often preached today. Jesus himself is the highest example of the motivation and purpose of all giving. He gave because he loved and he gave to bless.

The church does not need tithing to finance the work of God on earth. New Covenant giving is based on a better process. The born-again Christian is one with Christ and owned by him. His new nature is to live for Christ with all of his heart, mind, soul, strength, and money.

The following list includes some of the scriptural exhortations and perspectives related to giving in the New Testament. These can be applied to financial giving in the church today. Many of these are often overlooked because of the preoccupation with using the Old Covenant principle of tithing to motivate people.

1. To give glory to God.
    Matthew 5:16; 2 Corinthians 9:13.

2. To express the nature of God.
    Matthew 5:42, 45; Luke 6:35; 2 Corinthians 9:9.

3. You have freely received.
    Matthew 10:8; 2 Corinthians 9:15.

4. The workman is worthy of his hire.
    Matthew 10:10; Luke 10:7; 1 Corinthians 9:4–14; 2 Corinthians 11:8.

5. It's a family responsibility.
    Matthew 15:3–6; Mark 7:9–13; 1 Timothy 5:8–16.

6. To show compassion.
    Matthew 15:32, 18:27; Mark 8:2.

7. To have treasure in heaven.
    Matthew 19:21; Mark 10:21; Luke 12:33, 14:12–14, 18:22.

8. Do it as unto the Lord.
    Matthew 25:40,45; Luke 8:3, 19:31; Colossians 3:23.

9. To follow the example of Jesus.
    Mark 8:34–35; Luke 9:23–24; Ephesians 5:2.

10. To obey the Lord.
    Luke 6:30; 2 Corinthians 9:12–13.

11. It shall be given unto you.
    Luke 6:38; 2 Corinthians 9:6–11; Galatians
    6:7–9; Ephesians 6:8; Philippians 4:10–19.

12. To keep a pure heart.
    Luke 11:41; 1 Timothy 6:10.

13. To be a good steward.
    Matthew 25:14–30; Luke 12:42–48, 16:9–13, 19:
    12–26; 1 Corinthians 4:2; 1 Peter 4:9–10.

14. To promote God's kingdom.
    Luke 18:29; Philippians 1:3–5; 2 Corinthians
    8:1–5, 11:7–9.

15. To show love for the brethren and all men.
    Acts 11:29; 2 Corinthians 8:8, 24; 1 John 3:16–18,
    4:11; 3 John 5–6.

16. To support the weak.
    Acts 20:35; Galatians 6:2; 1 Timothy 5:16;
    James 1:27, 2:15–16.

17. It's more blessed to give than to receive.
    Acts 20:35.

18. It's an obligation to those who minister to you.
     Romans 15:25–27; 1 Corinthians 9:11; Galatians
     6:6; 1 Timothy 5:17–18; 2 Timothy 2:6.

19. It's a response to the grace of God.
     1 Corinthians 16:1–3; 2 Corinthians 8:1–9.

20. To minister to the other members of the body.
     2 Corinthians 8:4, 9:1; Galatians 6:10;
     Ephesians 4:28.

21. For a future reciprocation.
     2 Corinthians 8:14–15.

22. As you purpose in your heart.
     2 Corinthians 9:7.

23. It's a good work that we were created for.
     Ephesians 2:10; 1 Timothy 6:17–18; Titus 3:8, 14;
     Hebrews 13:16; James 2:14–26.

24. To bear fruit.
     John 15:1–16; Romans 15:28; Philippians 4:17;
     Colossians 1:10.

25. To keep our trust in God.
     Mark 10:23–25; Philippians 4:19; 1 Timothy
     6:17.

26. To enter into the true life.
     1 Timothy 6:19.

7

DISINFORMATION I

DISINFORMATION is false information, purposely given out to deceive an enemy. It's an ancient weapon of strategic warfare. The church is in a spiritual war and faces a steady stream of disinformation designed to deceive it and hold it in weakness. Jesus said that knowing the truth is the key to victory.

> And ye shall know the truth, and the truth shall make you free. (John 8:32)

The truth that will make you free is the knowledge of the finished work of Christ—his death, burial, resurrection, and what he accomplished by them. When a person understands identification with Christ, union with Christ, and living by the power of the indwelling Christ, he will have the spiritual foundation to experience the triumph of Christ. The devil tries to obscure that truth in his effort to neutralize the church.

Tithing contradicts the foundations of the New Covenant and life in Christ. It promotes a mentality that holds Christians in spiritual immaturity and weakness. The problem with tithing is not the percentage; it's the spiritual perspective that causes people to think, to believe, and to act inconsistently with the truth of what God has done through Christ and their relationship to him as a son.

In this chapter and the two following it we will examine some of the teachings on tithing that negate the truth. There are some you may have never heard before and some may even seem hard to believe, but they have all been preached by prominent and well-respected ministers.

THE TITHE IS THE LORD'S

This statement implies that tithing is an eternal law in God's kingdom that will never change. It is based on the following verses from the Old Testament.

> And all the tithe of the land, whether of the seed of the land, or of the fruit of the tree, is the LORD'S: it is holy unto the LORD. (Lev. 27:30)

> And concerning the tithe of the herd, or of the flock, even of whatsoever passeth under the rod, the tenth shall be holy unto the LORD. (Lev. 27:32)

Let's look at these verses in their context. Who is talking, who are they talking to, and what are they talking about? From verses 1 and 2 of the chapter we have the answer to all three questions. The Lord is speaking to Moses and is giving him instructions to give to the children of Israel. These instructions are not to the body of Christ. They are specifically for the people who lived under the Law. There is no tithe in the New Covenant so they cannot apply to us.

> Now we know that what things soever the law saith, it saith to them who are under the law: (Rom. 3:19)

The Law is not speaking to the new creation in Christ. It was never intended for us. We live in a much higher and better relationship with God.

> Wherefore the law was our schoolmaster to bring us unto Christ, that we might be justified by faith. But after that faith is come, we are no longer under a schoolmaster. (Gal. 3:24–25)

In the New Covenant we are sons of God. We are joint heirs with Jesus of all things. Jesus owns everything in both the seen and unseen worlds, and we are joint owners with him. This covenant is like a marriage, where 100 percent is owned by both parties and is at all times committed to the other's use.

Some believers who tithe have the wrong idea that 10 percent belongs to God and 90 percent belongs to them. But to walk with God you must accept his right to call for any amount at any time. Life in the spirit as a mature son is only available on that basis. With maturity comes both liberty and responsibility. We are to be led by the Holy Spirit, not by carnal principles like tithing that were necessary for men who were not born again.

People who have wrong beliefs about tithing can still be greatly blessed, according to their faith and how they follow the leading of the Holy Spirit. But no matter how blessed and successful they are, it doesn't validate their doctrine and it doesn't mean they have all that God has made available. The glorious life of Christ cannot be fully experienced while following a way of life that was intended for men who lived before the resurrection.

Most of the erroneous teaching on tithing comes from one thing; people are trying to apply Old Covenant principles to life in Christ and the two don't mix. Paul had his biggest problem with people who were trying to fit the New Covenant believers into an obsolete way of living. The same problem continues today.

People who teach tithing say they are not promoting the Law. However, the only instructions on tithing that came from God came through the Law to people who were under the Law. That was the only group of people he ever instructed to tithe.

The next four topics will cover one of the most often quoted passages on the subject of tithing, Malachi 3:8–11. It is another Old Covenant passage that is being wrongly applied to life in Christ.

IF YOU DON'T TITHE YOU ARE A GOD-ROBBER

> Will a man rob God? Yet ye have robbed me. But ye say, Wherein have we robbed thee? In tithes and offerings. (Mal. 3:8)

Under the Old Covenant the tithe was the Lord's and the children of Israel were robbing God when they didn't give it to him. We have a completely different relationship to God. The New Covenant is actually between God the Father and Jesus. Therefore, it is perfect and eternal because it does not depend on a fallible human who might break it. We are included in the New Covenant by our spiritual union with Jesus and we share his covenant relationship with the Father.

The Father has already given everything there is to the Son. Jesus Christ is the rightful Lord and owner of all things. By virtue of being in Christ and being his body we are joint owners of all things with him.

> For the promise, that he should be the heir of the world, was not to Abraham, or to his seed, through the law, but through the righteousness of faith. (Rom. 4:13)

> Now to Abraham and his seed were the promises made. He saith not, And to seeds, as of many; but as of one, And to thy seed, which is Christ. (Gal. 3:16)

> And if ye be Christ's, then are ye Abraham's seed,
> and heirs according to the promise. (Gal. 3:29)

> Therefore let no man glory in men. For all things
> are yours; Whether Paul, or Apollos, or Cephas, or
> the world, or life, or death, or things present, or
> things to come; all are yours; And ye are Christ's;
> and Christ is God's. (1 Cor. 3:21–23)

We have no possessions that are ours separately from
Jesus Christ. Everything belongs to him and us together, so
there is no such thing as robbing God by not tithing. The
commitment in this covenant is 100 percent from both parties. The issue is not tithing; it's following the Holy Spirit's
leading at all times.

Our relationship to God as a born-again son is superior
to anything previous. We are not our own, we have been
bought with a price, the blood of Jesus. God is not his own
either because he has committed himself to us, to be a
Father and total savior to us. We no longer live on the level
of a tither. We live in the high calling of absolute abandonment to God and his purposes on earth. That is the new
standard of 100 percent commitment in the New Covenant.

> So likewise, whosoever he be of you that forsaketh
> not all that he hath, he cannot be my disciple. (Luke
> 14:33)

> …they loved not their lives unto the death. (Rev. 12:11b)

The church is like it is today because of what it has been
taught. It has not been taught the strong truth about the

glorious relationship we have with God. It's time that Christians should be given the meat of God's word. (Heb. 5:12–14) It's time for them to be treated like sons who are capable of growing up into full stature in Christ.

Our standard today is not 10 percent, it is Christ himself who gave everything. Paul is an example for us:

> But what things were gain to me, those I counted loss for Christ. Yea doubtless, and I count all things but loss for the excellency of the knowledge of Christ Jesus my Lord: for whom I have suffered the loss of all things, and do count them but dung, that I may win Christ, (Phil. 3:7–8)

A CURSE WILL COME ON YOU IF YOU DON'T TITHE

> Ye are cursed with a curse: for ye have robbed me, even this whole nation. (Mal. 3:9)

God had given Israel the Law over one thousand years before the prophet Malachi spoke those words. God told Israel very clearly what the blessing would be for keeping the Law and what the curse would be for breaking it. Over the years Israel broke it repeatedly and suffered the curse as punishment. That was the nature of their covenant.

There is no curse upon us in Christ. It isn't part of our covenant. Jesus bore it and completely redeemed us from it.

> Christ hath redeemed us from the curse of the law,
> being made a curse for us: for it is written, Cursed
> is every one that hangeth on a tree: (Gal. 3:13)

Those who teach that there is a curse for not tithing are contradicting the most basic truths of the New Covenant. However, if you put yourself back under the Law you will put yourself under the curse.

> For as many as are of the works of the law are
> under the curse: for it is written, Cursed is every
> one that continueth not in all things which are writ-
> ten in the book of the law to do them. (Gal. 3:10)

Life in Christ works by a different spiritual process, which is not compatible with the Old Covenant paradigm.

> Therefore it is of faith, that it might be by grace; to
> the end the promise might be sure to all the seed;
> (Rom. 4:16)

WE ARE COMMANDED TO PROVE GOD WITH THE TITHE

> Bring ye all the tithes into the storehouse, that there
> may be meat in mine house, and prove me now
> herewith, saith the LORD of hosts, if I will not open
> you the windows of heaven, and pour you out a
> blessing, that there shall not be room enough to
> receive it. (Mal. 3:10)

Just as there was a curse for breaking the Law, there was a blessing for keeping the Law. Israel was challenged to keep the law of tithing and thereby put God to the test. Malachi 3:10 was not written to the church.

We are operating from a completely different perspective. God has already given us everything in our union with Christ. We don't do things to earn blessings. Neither is there a curse upon us if we fall short. God is looking for mature sons who will abide in Christ and allow him to live through them. God wants us to walk by faith and follow the leading of the Holy Spirit, not tithe.

The mind we have in Christ is a consciousness of already having all needs met, even though the provision may not be seen in the natural realm. That is faith. The idea that giving will cause God to do something is not faith, it's a mentality of lack and manipulation. When giving is based on love for people and faith that God has already provided for you, then it's in agreement with the truth

The New Covenant doesn't operate by generic standards like the tithe. It is administrated by the Holy Spirit in a way that is unique to each person and situation. Jesus told the rich young ruler to sell everything, give the money to the poor, and come follow him. (Matt. 19:16–30, Luke 18:18–30) Those instructions were unique to him. A tithe would not have been sufficient.

In 1 Timothy 6:17–18 the rich are not commanded to give everything away like the rich young ruler was. They are instructed how they should use their wealth. When Peter asked Jesus what would be required of John, he was told that it was none of his business. (John 21:20–22) God deals with each person and situation individually.

There are many ways that faith can be expressed; however, they will all be uniquely inspired by the Holy Spirit for the specific situation. Faith is what God is looking for now, not tithing.

> But without faith it is impossible to please him: for he that cometh to God must believe that he is, and that he is a rewarder of them that diligently seek him. (Heb. 11:6)

> So then they which be of faith are blessed with faithful Abraham. (Gal. 3:9)

The difference between faith and works is a matter of the heart. Something that's done to get a blessing is a work. Something that's done because you believe you already have all blessings is an action of faith. Grace and works do not mix. Either we are blessed as a free gift of grace or we are blessed because of our works.

> Now to him that worketh is the reward not reckoned of grace, but of debt. But to him that worketh not, but believeth on him that justifieth the ungodly, his faith is counted for righteousness. (Rom. 4:4–5)

> And if by grace, then is it no more of works: otherwise grace is no more grace. But if it be of works, then is it no more grace: otherwise work is no more work. (Rom. 11:6)

Tithing Rebukes the Devourer

> And I will rebuke the devourer for your sakes, and
> he shall not destroy the fruits of your ground; nei-
> ther shall your vine cast her fruit before the time in
> the field, saith the LORD of hosts. (Mal. 3:11)

God promised to rebuke the devourer if Israel would keep their covenant obligation to tithe. If they didn't, the curse of destruction would come on them.

Again, the New Covenant operates differently than the Old. Jesus has already defeated the devil, redeemed us from his works, and delivered us out of his authority. It's all based on Jesus' shed blood, not on tithing. We are not waiting for God to rebuke the devourer. Jesus has given us the authority and the responsibility to use his name to enforce his finished work.

The New Testament graphically describes the devil's defeat and Jesus' triumph.

> And having spoiled principalities and powers, he
> made a shew of them openly, triumphing over
> them in it. (Col. 2:15)

> Forasmuch then as the children are partakers of
> flesh and blood, he also himself likewise took part
> of the same; that through death he might destroy
> him that had the power of death, that is, the devil;
> And deliver them who through fear of death were
> all their lifetime subject to bondage. (Heb. 2:14–15)

> Which he wrought in Christ, when he raised him
> from the dead, and set him at his own right hand in
> the heavenly places, Far above all principality, and
> power, and might, and dominion, and every name
> that is named, not only in this world, but also in
> that which is to come: (Eph. 1:20–21)

The New Testament is very clear that everything Jesus
did in his death, burial, and resurrection was for our benefit and that we now share his complete victory and authority over all the power of darkness.

> Even when we were dead in sins, hath quickened
> us together with Christ, (by grace ye are saved;)
> And hath raised us up together, and made us sit
> together in heavenly places in Christ Jesus: (Eph. 2:
> 5–6)

> Giving thanks unto the Father, which hath made us
> meet to be partakers of the inheritance of the saints
> in light: Who hath delivered us from the power of
> darkness, and hath translated us into the kingdom
> of his dear Son: In whom we have redemption
> through his blood, even the forgiveness of sins:
> (Col. 1:12–14)

> For in him dwelleth all the fulness of the Godhead
> bodily. And ye are complete in him, which is the
> head of all principality and power: (Col. 2:9–10)

Through Christ we are in a place of victory and authority that was unknown to the people of God in previous
covenants. God had servants under the Law, and if they

kept the Law he could bless them. God now has sons in Christ and expects a different way of living from them. He has given us a staggering amount of authority in the name of Jesus and the responsibility that goes with it.

> Verily I say unto you, Whatsoever ye shall bind on earth shall be bound in heaven: and whatsoever ye shall loose on earth shall be loosed in heaven. (Matt. 18:18)

> Behold, I give unto you power (authority) to tread on serpents and scorpions, and over all the power of the enemy: and nothing shall by any means hurt you. (Luke 10:19)

> And Jesus came and spake unto them, saying, All power (authority) is given unto me in heaven and in earth. (Matt. 28:18)

> And these signs shall follow them that believe; In my name shall they cast out devils; they shall speak with new tongues; They shall take up serpents; and if they drink any deadly thing, it shall not hurt them; they shall lay hands on the sick, and they shall recover. (Mark 16:17–18)

> Wherefore God also hath highly exalted him, and given him a name which is above every name: That at the name of Jesus every knee should bow, of things in heaven, and things in earth, and things under the earth; And that every tongue should confess that Jesus Christ is Lord, to the glory of God the Father. (Phil. 2:9–11)

God is not waiting to rebuke the devourer for those who tithe; he has already thrashed him! Any man in Christ has the benefit of that total victory without tithing. Putting people's attention on tithing as the source of their protection from the devil is a deception. It keeps them in a weak, Old Covenant mindset. It distracts them from their responsibility to bind the devil and cast him out in Jesus name.

THE TITHE IS THE CONNECTION
TO THE COVENANT

Tithing has been wrongly exalted beyond the actual importance that it did have in the Old Covenant. Sometimes it seems that tithing has become the paramount issue in Christian preaching and teaching. However, in the covenant that God made with Israel at Mt. Sinai, tithing was just one of the Law's many requirements.

In God's covenant with Abraham, tithing was not included. God guaranteed that covenant without any requirement of tithing. Tithing is not part of the New Covenant either. It is based on the blood of Jesus alone.

> For this is my blood of the new testament, which is shed for many for the remission of sins. (Matt. 26:28)

> Of how much sorer punishment, suppose ye, shall he be thought worthy, who hath trodden under foot the Son of God, and hath counted the blood of

the covenant, wherewith he was sanctified, an unholy thing, and hath done despite unto the Spirit of grace? (Heb. 10:29)

God knew that the only way to provide salvation and blessing to man was to provide it as a free gift. Man was incapable of contributing anything. Jesus provided all that was required, his own shed blood. Salvation is by grace and it includes every benefit purchased by the blood of Jesus at the cross. If prosperity or any other covenant blessing depended on the tithe, then the tithe would be purchasing it, not the blood of Jesus.

The New Covenant is a blood covenant not a tithe covenant. Faith is the connection, but it is faith in the shed blood of Jesus, not faith in tithing. Making tithing a requirement to maintain the covenant is just as wrong as making it a requirement to enter the covenant.

8

DISINFORMATION II

JESUS TITHED

It is said that Jesus tithed. The Bible doesn't say so specifically, but people are quick to assume he did because he lived during the Law. That is the root of the whole tithing error: careless assumption based on faulty premises. It produces dysfunctional religious doctrine and a weak church.

Unless Jesus had agricultural produce from the land, increase from fields, vineyards, orchards, flocks, herds, and beehives, which were designated by the Law to be tithed on, he would not have been tithing. Even if he gave 10 percent of his carpentry income or a tenth of his ministry offerings, it would not have been called the "tithe" according to the Law's definition. We know that he gave to the poor, but he would not have been focusing on a percentage. That would be irrelevant to the principle of freewill offerings and to the spirit of giving.

Whether Jesus tithed or not, it has nothing to do with how a born-again son of God is supposed to live in the New Covenant. Jesus would have done a lot of things during that Old Covenant time period which he never intended for his church to do. If tithing was as important as we are told that it is, Jesus would have emphasized it in his own life and teaching. On the contrary, he minimized its importance by barely mentioning it.

Jesus was the divine nature of God in operation. His standard of life was so far above the Law that there was no comparison. The same should be true of the church, which is his body on earth. Our way of living and giving today should be far above anything previous, including both the Law and Abraham. When the church sees the truth of life in Christ it will be transformed. All previous giving will look weak and beggarly compared to what it will then do.

JESUS TAUGHT TITHING

It is said that Jesus taught tithing. If so, to whom did he teach it? In Matthew 23:23 and Luke 11:42 Jesus acknowledged to the Pharisees that tithing was their duty, but he rebuked them for passing over the more important parts of the Law which were judgement, mercy, faith, and the love of God. In Luke 18:9–14 Jesus told a parable of two men going to the temple to pray. One was a self-righteous

Pharisee who bragged to God about fasting twice a week and giving tithes of all he possessed. The other was a publican who said, "God be merciful to me a sinner." Jesus said the publican went down to his house justified rather than the Pharisee. None of these incidents were emphasizing the importance of tithing.

Jesus merely confirmed that the people he was speaking to were under the Law and that tithing was a part of their covenant obligation. He was not giving instructions to the New Covenant believer. There is no other record of Jesus talking about tithing. His relative silence on the subject tells us that it is not the key to blessing and prosperity in the New Covenant.

The New Covenant was going to be such a radical change in relationship to God that there was very little Jesus could say about it at the time. The people couldn't understand it. He told his disciples in John 16:12–13:

> I have yet many things to say unto you, but ye cannot bear them now. Howbeit when he, the Spirit of truth, is come, he will guide you into all truth: for he shall not speak of himself; but whatsoever he shall hear, that shall he speak: and he will shew you things to come.

God has put his own nature in the born-again Christian. When the church gets a revelation of their union with Christ they will start living to serve God. They will have to be told to stop giving instead of having to be constantly harangued to start giving.

THE TITHE REDEEMS THE OTHER NINETY PERCENT

To say that paying a tithe is what protects the remaining 90 percent from a curse of destruction is contrary to the New Covenant and it devaluates the blood of Jesus. Money can't redeem anything and neither can the practice of tithing.

> In whom we have redemption through his blood, even the forgiveness of sins: (Col. 1:14)

> Neither by the blood of goats and calves, but by his own blood he entered in once into the holy place, having obtained eternal redemption for us. (Heb. 9:12)

> Forasmuch as ye know that ye were not redeemed with corruptible things, as silver and gold, from your vain conversation received by tradition from your fathers; But with the precious blood of Christ, as of a lamb without blemish and without spot: (1 Pet. 1:18–19)

In the New Covenant we are redeemed. It is a finished work. It doesn't have to be redone each time we get a paycheck. Satan is defeated. We are not in his jurisdiction. We are not under the curse. The blood of Jesus paid the total price for our deliverance and there is nothing we can do to add to it.

Redemption means that God has purchased us and owns us. He has rightful claim to everything about us: ourselves, our time, our money, and every detail of our lives.

He expresses his will to each person individually through the working of the Holy Spirit, not on the basis of the tithe.

One aspect of the wisdom and superiority of the New Covenant is that the Holy Spirit can direct each person's life uniquely for any circumstance. The Law was complex because it had to address a wide range of events that might occur. The religious leaders in Israel made additions to cover even more situations. The Holy Spirit in the New Covenant has made things simple. He will direct each person individually to deal with anything they face in life, including giving money and supporting the work of God's kingdom on earth.

Paul said in Galatians 5:1:

> Stand fast therefore in the liberty wherewith Christ hath made us free, and be not entangled again with the yoke of bondage.

Well-meaning people will try to constrain you with a yoke of religious bondage. You must know the truth in Christ to be free and stay free.

TITHING QUALIFIES YOU TO RECEIVE MORE FROM GOD

This statement is based on the belief that tithing is one of the foundational principles of faithful financial stewardship for Christians today. But there is no scriptural basis for that thinking. Financial stewardship in the New Covenant is based on following the leading of the Holy Spirit, who deals with each member of the body of Christ individually. The Holy Spirit has the wisdom and knowledge to be prepared for any need that arises, any time and any place. Much giving will be regular and dependable but the Holy Spirit is the one who determines what is best in every situation. He reserves the right to interrupt the status quo. The church needs to learn to trust him. He will do a far better job than the principle of tithing.

The New Covenant has ended the compartmentalization of life. No part is more spiritual than another. In God's family enterprise we are expected to live for him with all of our resources, not just money. But in regard to stewardship, financial giving has been over-emphasized as the most important aspect. There are many other aspects of stewardship that are completely ignored. One that is almost unheard of is being led by the Holy Spirit not to give.

The goal of stewardship is to use all resources wisely by the infinite wisdom and knowledge of the Holy Spirit. It is not to just give more and more and more. It is not to give money in every meeting or to put something in every offering plate that passes by. If our giving is based on fulfilling an obligation like the tithe or on working a principle for our own financial benefit, we may be giving money at times and at places that we shouldn't be.

God doesn't want us to put valuable resources into something that he isn't directing. Even if some project or ministry is ordained by God, he may want someone else to support it so that we will have resources available for another particular purpose that he knows is coming in the future. Recognizing the Holy Spirit's guidance when he tells us not to give is also part of good stewardship.

"HONOR THE LORD WITH YOUR SUBSTANCE AND WITH THE FIRSTFRUITS OF ALL YOUR INCREASE" MEANS TO TITHE

This statement comes from Proverb 3:9–10:

> Honour the LORD with thy substance, and with the firstfruits of all thine increase: So shall thy barns be filled with plenty, and thy presses shall burst out with new wine.

Solomon was speaking first of all to the people of his day who were living under the Law as he was. It does have an application to us today, but it isn't to tithe.

There were many ways for a person to honor God with their substance under the Law. Some were commandments and some were voluntary. Tithing was just one of the many financial aspects of the Law.

Firstfruits was a distinctly different offering than the tithe. It was voluntary and had no set amount for its size. However, there were specific instructions regarding when it was to be done, in what form it was to be brought, in what manner it was to be offered, and how it was to be used. Honoring the Lord with your firstfruits had nothing to do with tithing.

This verse is a reminder to us that all material wealth is a blessing from God. Using material resources for his kingdom is part of our nature as sons. We can expect the blessings of God to be upon us as we abide in Christ and live for him by faith. As Paul said in 2 Corinthians 9:6–8:

> But this I say, He which soweth sparingly shall reap also sparingly; and he which soweth bountifully shall reap also bountifully.
>
> Every man according as he purposeth in his heart, so let him give; not grudgingly, or of necessity: for God loveth a cheerful giver.
>
> And God is able to make all grace abound toward you; that ye, always having all sufficiency in all things, may abound to every good work:

Tithing Puts God First in Your Life

Many people tithe because they love themselves, not God. They have been convinced that a curse will come on them if they don't tithe and that a blessing will come on them if they do. So they tithe faithfully, but God is not first. And as already said, God is not impressed with being first. He expects to be all and that can only happen by the power of the Holy Spirit, when a person gets a revelation of what the gospel really means. People who are trying to put God first in their lives, by tithing or anything else, do not have a revelation of life in Christ in the New Covenant. When they get it they will be transformed and their giving will be an expression of the love of God in their heart.

THE TITHE MUST BE THE FIRST CHECK WRITTEN

This teaching is a combination of two separate concepts in the Old Covenant: the "Law of First Things" and the "Law of the Tithe." The resulting hybrid law has been brought over into the New Covenant and applied to the church. Besides violating the New, this hybrid is also a faulty interpretation of the Old.

The "Law of First Things" is a reference to the commandments about the firstborn of man and animal and the firstfruits of fields, vineyards, and oliveyards. It is a separate concept from tithing and was regulated by separate commandments. God had no tolerance for changes in the Law. He designed each aspect to teach a spiritual lesson.

The Law said in Exodus 13:2:

> Sanctify unto me all the firstborn, whatsoever openeth the womb among the children of Israel, both of man and of beast: it is mine.

That was a one-time event for an individual animal. The tithe was an annual event from the herd as a whole. The two concepts couldn't be combined. There were two separate laws for two separate purposes and spiritual lessons.

Another unscriptural statement that has become popular is, "If it's not first, it's not a tithe." That means if you spend anything before you pay the tithe then you have violated God's law and there will be no blessing. But the farmers in Israel couldn't know what their tithe would be until the entire harvest was finished. After that there was still a period of time before it could be delivered to the storehouse. In the meantime there was no law against selling or using the portion that belonged to them. God didn't burden them with excessive legalism.

The Bible also contradicts that teaching in another way. According to the Law, when taking a tithe of flocks and herds, the tenth one that passed under the rod was the one given to the Lord, not the first one.

> And concerning the tithe of the herd, or of the flock, even of whatsoever passeth under the rod, the tenth shall be holy unto the LORD.
>
> He shall not search whether it be good or bad, neither shall he change it: and if he change it at all, then both it and the change thereof shall be holy; it shall not be redeemed. (Lev. 27:32–33)

The word "tenth" in Leviticus 27:32 is an ordinal number, meaning the tenth one in a sequence. It does not mean a tithe or 10 percent. It comes from a different Hebrew word. That means the tenth animal belonged to the Lord, not the first one.

Israel was also instructed not to inspect the tenth animal to see if it was good or bad. It didn't matter if it was a bad one; that is the one they were commanded to give and they were not to replace it with a good one. That is another example of the Law being different than what we have been taught about it.

It must be said repeatedly, the key to the question of tithing is getting a revelation of New Covenant life in Christ. Without a revelation of that, people get bogged down in controversy over isolated scriptures and miss the real issue. Sincere people are trying to fit New Covenant living into a framework of Old Testament types and shadows. Jesus gave Paul the apostle a revelation of spiritual reality in the New Covenant. All types and shadows need to be interpreted in the light of that.

Bringing the law of tithing over into the New Covenant is wrong in itself. Creating a new hybrid law, out of tithing and firstfruits, and adding it on top of tithing is the same as what the Pharisees did. The Law wasn't extensive enough for them. They had another body of law that they had created and added to God's law. In their minds they were sincere but they missed the point.

People don't think that the doctrine of tithing is a message of righteousness by works. But if all of God's redemption, protection, and blessing depend on tithing, then what good is the righteousness we have been given as a free gift? They don't mean to say it but the righteousness they leave us with isn't good for anything by itself. So it isn't righteousness at all.

If failure to tithe makes me a God-robber, then my right-eousness depends on tithing. If failure to write out the first check on payday to the local church causes me to lose the favor of God on my life, then my righteousness must depend on doing that. If tithing is what redeems the remaining 90 percent of my paycheck, then the blood of Jesus did not redeem it. If a curse is going to come upon me for not tithing, then Christ has not redeemed me from the curse of the Law.

The popular teaching on tithing is really saying that we need Christ plus tithing. It is saying that the blood of Jesus wasn't enough, that we need the blood plus tithing. The message of grace and the message of tithing are as different as night and day.

9

DISINFORMATION III

TITHING BEGAN IN THE GARDEN OF EDEN

Some people say that tending to the tree of the knowledge of good and evil without being able to eat of its fruit is the same principle as the tithe. They want to show that Adam and Eve were tithing in the garden of Eden to prove that tithing is an eternal principle, still in effect today.

The tree was the focal point for the issue of obedience to God; however, calling the tree a tithe is another distortion of the scripture. People have read something into the Bible that isn't there because they haven't understood the nature of New Covenant life in Christ and they are looking for something to validate and promote the doctrine of tithing.

WHEN JESUS DIED ON THE CROSS, GOD WAS PAYING HIS TITHE

Most people have never heard this statement, but it has become popular among some well-respected ministries. It sounds scriptural and at first it doesn't seem to violate the gospel message, but it distorts the meaning of both the cross and the tithe. It's an inaccurate parallel that is used to promote tithing. It seems relatively harmless, but it is part of a serious theological error that has produced a church that is weak and ineffective, by God's standards.

When Jesus died on the cross, he was fulfilling the eternal plan of God that existed before creation. He was "the Lamb slain from the foundation of the world." (Rev. 13:8b) His death on the cross was also God's fulfillment of a promise to Abraham. God had tested Abraham's faith and commitment by commanding him to offer his son Isaac as a sacrifice. Abraham passed the test and the event became God's prophetic picture of his own covenant obligation to offer Jesus as a sacrifice for man's salvation.

Jesus' death was a fulfillment of God's covenant commitment but it had nothing to do with a tithe. When Abraham offered up Isaac it had nothing to do with a tithe either. Isaac was 100 percent of all that Abraham had because the rest of his wealth was worthless compared to his son. A tithe is a tenth and it leaves you with 90 percent. Abraham was giving everything when he offered Isaac.

Likewise, when the Father gave Jesus it was everything on his part as well. Colossians 2:9 says, "For in him dwelleth all the fulness of the Godhead bodily." Jesus Christ was the full expression of God and everything that he could give, not just a tithe.

Tithes are based on the increase of something that has already been received. God gave in advance, before he received anything. He gave without any guarantees. He gave without regard to whether anyone would accept the sacrifice of Jesus or not. He gave because it is his nature.

God didn't owe a tithe to us or to himself. We owed him a debt that we could never pay. The message of the cross is that Jesus was there in our place, on our behalf. He was doing something for us that we could not do for ourselves. So if God was paying anyone's tithe it would not have been his, it would have been ours.

Paul did describe the resurrected Lord Jesus Christ as the firstfruits.

> But now is Christ risen from the dead, and become
> the firstfruits of them that slept. (1 Cor. 15:20)

However, a firstfruits offering is a completely different Old Covenant offering than the tithe. The *how, when,* and *why* of a firstfruits offering is based on a different concept and the two are not interchangeable. God made tithes and first-fruits distinctly different so that they would portray different spiritual lessons. Beyond that, in describing Jesus as the firstfruits, Paul was talking about his resurrection not his death. There is no sound scriptural basis to call Jesus' death on the cross a tithe. That is a faulty parallel. It is a mislead-ing concept that reinforces the erroneous tithing doctrine.

IF YOU DON'T TITHE, GOD WILL TAKE THAT TEN PERCENT FROM YOU

Some say it this way, "God will get what is his." This teaching is based on the idea that God owns a tenth of everything that comes to you. If you don't tithe, you are a thief in possession of stolen property and God will take it from you to teach you a lesson. I heard a story about a person who didn't tithe one week and then had a situation occur that cost them exactly what their tithe would have been.

The word of God should be the basis of our faith and our doctrine, not someone's experience. Everything in that teaching is contrary to what the Bible clearly says about the New Covenant. Since his resurrection, the Lord Jesus Christ is the absolute owner of all things, not just the tithe. Jesus purchased us with his blood and we belong to him as well. But that is not the end of the story. When we were born again we were placed into spiritual union with Jesus and we now jointly own all things with him.

We have no stolen property because we share rightful title to everything with Jesus. On the other hand 100 percent of it is dedicated to his lordship and the purposes of his kingdom, not just a tenth. He doesn't want a tithe. He wants people who will use everything they have for him.

Those who don't know the truth about life in Christ are subject to whatever wrong teaching they hear. If they think they will be cursed for not tithing, their own fear will open a door to destruction. They can't receive God's blessing and protection if they think they are breaking his law.

We are in a new, joyous, spiritual relationship with God that only includes freewill giving. 2 Corinthians 9:7 says,

> Every man according as he purposeth in his heart, so let him give; not grudgingly, or of necessity: for God loveth a cheerful giver.

If God was holding curses over people's heads he couldn't have truly cheerful givers because they would be giving under duress.

IF EVERYONE TITHED, CHURCHES WOULD HAVE PLENTY OF MONEY

Churches and ministries do need money and they would have more than they have now if everyone tithed, but tithing is not God's solution for the problem.

We need to step back and ask ourselves why preaching the doctrine of tithing isn't working. Why do so few Christians tithe in spite of the endless haranguing to do so? The Barna Research Group's nationwide survey of donations indicates that only 14 percent of born-again Christians in the continental United States gave at least ten percent of their income in 2001.[1] Instead of beating our heads against the wall, we should see if our theology is in agreement with the word of God.

Mark 16:20 indicates that Jesus confirms the preaching of his word with signs following. But tithing is not the plan of God for the New Covenant and Jesus is not confirming that message. The Holy Spirit can't do a work of grace in the hearts of people to obey a teaching that isn't grace or truth. If the true message of the New Covenant and life in union with Christ would be preached, we would see the Holy Spirit move in the church. There would be enough financial giving to do anything the Lord directs. There would be a completely new spirit of revival as well.

Heaven Will Be Shut Up Against You If You Don't Tithe

The Old Covenant declared that a curse would come on Israel if they broke God's law. In Leviticus 26:19 God said he would make their heaven as iron and in Deuteronomy 28:23 he said it would be brass. Naturally speaking, lack of rain for crops and livestock would be a devastating punishment. It was spiritually symbolic too. There would be no answer to their prayers as a result of their disobedience.

This teaching about heaven being shut up against God's people if they don't tithe also comes from Malachi 3 where God is rebuking the nation of Israel for breaking the covenant. In verse 10 he says:

> Bring ye all the tithes into the storehouse, that there may be meat in mine house, and prove me now herewith, saith the LORD of hosts, if I will not open you the windows of heaven, and pour you out a blessing, that there shall not be room enough to receive it.

Israel wasn't giving God the tithes that were required by their covenant, so they were a nation of God-robbers and they were under a curse. God promised to open the windows of heaven for them if they would tithe because that was the cause of their problem. But tithing is not part of our covenant, so failure to tithe is not the source of our problems and tithing is not the solution for them.

MIRACLE TESTIMONIES PROVE THAT TITHING IS GOD'S WILL

There are many testimonies of God's miraculous provision for people who tithe. There are just as many testimonies of God's blessing and provision for people who live wholeheartedly for him without tithing. Christians who live blessed and prosperous lives without tithing are not publicized. No one has anything to gain by telling their story, so you hear nothing about them. Something else that is not publicized is the number of people who tithe regularly and are not receiving the financial provision that they should.

There are many things that affect the level of blessing and prosperity in a person's life. God looks at the heart. Sometimes people get an attitude corrected or move from unbelief to faith, which allows God to bless them, but they mistakenly attribute the blessing to something they have done, like tithing. When faithful tithers are not receiving a reasonable level of financial blessing they are told that they are still missing it somewhere else in their life—rightly so.

But when they get the other things corrected and start receiving God's provision, tithing still gets the credit.

People say, "I wouldn't stop tithing, I've done it too long and I know it works." They don't realize that God is good and gracious and he responds to faith where he can find it.

> For the eyes of the LORD run to and fro through-
> out the whole earth, to shew himself strong in the
> behalf of them whose heart is perfect toward him.
> (2 Chron. 16:9)

God blesses sincere people who put actions to their faith even though their theology may not be correct.

HOW WILL WE GET OUR NEEDS MET IF WE DON'T TITHE?

This question shows that some people think their tithe is what makes their provision come to them. They think God would stop causing it to come if they stopped tithing. They have more faith in a system they are working than they do in a God who has committed himself to be a Father to them. They don't understand that life in Christ is life as an immediate member of God's own family. Their relationship to God has been thoroughly systematized: built around programs and institutions. It is so corrupted by carnal religious inventions that they don't know how to walk with God as sons. They don't realize how well God is providing for millions of dedicated Christians who don't tithe.

Give Only to People and Ministries That Tithe or Your Seed Won't Multiply

This teaching comes partly from the faulty premise that the purpose of giving is to get a return and partly from theological invention. For many people, giving has become primarily a business venture because they don't understand the New Covenant.

There are many promises in the Bible about blessings coming to people who give and to people who help the poor but none of them require the recipient of the gift to be a tither. Jesus told the rich young ruler to sell all that he had and give it to the poor and that he would have treasure in heaven. He didn't say, "Make sure they are tithers or your seed won't multiply."

The largest passages in the New Testament epistles that refer to giving are talking about an offering that was being collected for the poor Christians in Jerusalem who were going through a famine. This was not a collection for full-time ministers. It was for all the poor people in the church. In regard to this offering, Paul said:

> But this I say, He which soweth sparingly shall reap also sparingly; and he which soweth bountifully shall reap also bountifully. (2 Cor. 9:6)

The blessing promised didn't depend on the recipient being a tither.

TWENTY-PERCENT PENALTY ON UNPAID TITHES

This teaching is rare but it shows how far some have gone in applying the Old Covenant to the New. The Law included a penalty of 20 percent for any trespass that related to the holy things of the Lord. (Lev. 5:15–16) If a person sinned through ignorance, they were to bring a ram for a sacrifice plus the value of the trespass in silver shekels and include a twenty-percent penalty.

I heard a story about a husband and wife who stopped tithing because they were having financial difficulties. They kept track of what it should have been and paid it later with interest. Their sincerity was admirable but they didn't have a revelation of New Covenant life in Christ.

STATEMENT FROM THE OLD TESTAMENT TO MAKE WHEN TITHING

Deuteronomy 26:1–15 instructed the Israelites what to say to the priest when they brought their firstfruits offerings and their tithes. (There were actually two separate offerings with two separate declarations.) Most preachers aren't legalistic about this. They are just drawing a parallel from the Old Covenant and applying it to us. However, its overall effect is to keep the church's attention on tithing. The greater error is that they are basing life in Christ on an obsolete, Old Covenant paradigm.

LEGALISTIC NATURE OF TITHING

Law by nature must be clear and specific. Therefore, it requires constant expansion and clarification to accurately apply it to all the different situations that continue to arise. The religious leaders in Israel added a great body of oral law to the Law that Moses received at Mt. Sinai.

Many preachers of tithing vigorously deny that they are preaching a law, but it fits the profile perfectly. There are as many opinions of how tithing should be done as there are preachers who promote it. This should be an indication to perceptive Christians that it is not the Holy Spirit's plan for us today.

Consider the following questions and issues that relate to tithing.

- Do you tithe on gross income before taxes or net income after taxes?

- Does the tithe have to be the very first thing paid when you receive income?

- Does the whole tithe have to go to your local church?

- Are you obligated to tithe if your spouse does not agree to it?

- Are you obligated to tithe if you have concerns about the financial stewardship by those in authority?

- How should the tithe be given by people in business who don't know what profits are until the end of the year or later?

- Do ministers tithe back to the church that pays them?

- ▸ Are ministries required to tithe to other ministries?

- ▸ What does a person do about back tithes that they failed to pay?

- ▸ Do people who aren't in full-time ministry tithe on money that is given to them for a missionary trip?

- ▸ What if you receive an inheritance of land or personal property but have no cash to pay a tithe on it? Are you required to sell it to pay the tithe? If you paid the tithe over time would you pay penalties and interest on it? Would you feel nervous about having God's full blessing and protection until the tithe was fully paid?

- ▸ Do you tithe on payments for child support?

- ▸ Do you tithe on insurance settlements for physical injury or property damage?

- ▸ Do you tithe on the value of non-monetary Social Security, welfare, or veteran's benefits?

- ▸ Do you tithe on the value of free day-care, health insurance, or other benefits that are provided by your employer?

- ▸ Do you tithe on the value of college scholarships and grants?

- ▸ Do you tithe on the value of gifts and prizes?

The fact that people have to ask so many questions about how to tithe shows that it is not an inward working of the Holy Spirit. It is not Christ in them that is motivating them to do it. They are trying to fulfill a law that they have been given.

10

RIGHTEOUSNESS

IF you have trusted in the Lord Jesus Christ and have called upon him for salvation, receiving him into your heart and life as Lord and Savior, then you are righteous. Your righteousness is more than just being forgiven of your sins. It is more than just being considered by God as someone who has never done anything wrong. You have the righteousness of someone who has also done everything right, someone who has done all of God's will, has kept all of his law, and has done it all to perfection. That is the righteousness of Christ, that is his perfect standing with the Father, and that is what you have through faith in him. Jesus' relationship to the Father is the definition of righteousness. There is no other kind. That is what you have and you have it now.

Your righteousness was a free gift from God. It was freely given without reservation. It was given by grace alone without any works or deeds on your part whatsoever. It was paid for by the shed blood of Jesus. You received it by faith. It is perfect righteousness. It is the right standing that Jesus Christ has with the Father. It causes the Father to treat you the same as Jesus. It includes all the benefits and privileges of Jesus' relationship to the Father. If it didn't it wouldn't be his righteousness. You have the privilege of accepting it or rejecting it but you do not have the privilege of changing any of its terms or features.

Your righteousness is more than a legal declaration. It is real. It has substance. The message of Paul's epistles is that we have been made to be the actual righteousness of God through Jesus Christ.

> For he hath made him to be sin for us, who knew no sin; that we might be made the righteousness of God in him. (2 Cor. 5:21)

> And that ye put on the new man, which after God is created in righteousness and true holiness. (Eph. 4:24)

That is the mystery of the gospel, how a man with a sinful nature can be spiritually reborn with the righteous nature of Jesus Christ. It is the story of identification and substitution. Jesus identified with us by first becoming a man and then by bearing our sin, our separation from God, and our curse in order to redeem us. He died a substitutionary death on the cross. He was there in our place.

Jesus was made alive and raised up from the realm of death and eternal judgement when our redemption had been accomplished. He was restored again to perfect standing with the Father, seated at his right hand. Salvation is an exchange. Our old identity and spiritual nature are crucified and put to death with Christ on the cross and we receive his resurrection nature and identity in exchange. By that we also receive his relationship to the Father.

Jesus revealed the mystery to Paul the apostle and inspired him to write it in his epistles. By the power of the Holy Spirit we can understand it and walk in it.

> But we speak the wisdom of God in a mystery, even the hidden wisdom, which God ordained before the world unto our glory: (1 Cor. 2:7)

> How that by revelation he made known unto me the mystery; (as I wrote afore in few words, Whereby, when ye read, ye may understand my knowledge in the mystery of Christ) (Eph. 3:3, 4)

The mystery begins with our spiritual union with Jesus Christ.

> For we are members of his body, of his flesh, and of his bones. ...This is a great mystery: but I speak concerning Christ and the church. (Eph. 5:30, 32)

> Even the mystery which hath been hid from ages and from generations, but now is made manifest to his saints: ...which is Christ in you, the hope of glory: (Col. 1:26, 27)

Everything that Jesus did at the cross was for us. His death, burial, and resurrection was an eternal event that was accomplished in the spirit realm, free from the limits of time and space. By the work of the Holy Spirit, any man who calls upon the Lord Jesus is supernaturally included with him in that event so that he may receive the results of what God was doing there for all mankind.

We are spiritually immersed into the being of Christ by the Holy Spirit. That is the meaning of baptism. Water baptism is an outward demonstration of what happens in the spiritual realm when a person is placed into Christ.

> For by one Spirit are we all baptized into one body,
> ...and have been all made to drink into one Spirit.
> (1 Cor. 12:13)

> For as many of you as have been baptized into Christ have put on Christ. (Gal. 3:27)

> But he that is joined unto the Lord is one spirit.
> (1 Cor. 6:17)

Our spiritual union with Christ began at the cross. It was there that he made the ultimate identification with us in our sin.

> Know ye not, that so many of us as were baptized into Jesus Christ were baptized into his death? (Rom. 6:3)

In every subsequent step of the redemptive process, we were included with Christ through the spiritual mystery of our union with him. We received the transforming effects of everything that God was doing in Christ as our substitute. Paul records each aspect as it was revealed to him by Jesus: crucifixion, death, burial, being made alive, being raised up, and being seated at the Father's right hand.

CRUCIFIED WITH CHRIST

> Knowing this, that our old man is crucified with him, that the body of sin might be destroyed, that henceforth we should not serve sin. (Rom. 6:6)

> I am crucified with Christ: (Gal. 2:20a)

> But God forbid that I should glory, save in the cross of our Lord Jesus Christ, by whom the world is crucified unto me, and I unto the world. (Gal. 6:14)

DEAD WITH CHRIST

> For the love of Christ constraineth us; because we thus judge, that if one died for all, then were all dead: (2 Cor. 5:14)

> Now if we be dead with Christ, we believe that we shall also live with him: (Rom. 6:8)

> Wherefore if ye be dead with Christ (Col. 2:20a)

> For ye are dead, and your life is hid with Christ in God. (Col. 3:3)

> It is a faithful saying: For if we be dead with him, we shall also live with him: (2 Tim. 2:11)

BURIED WITH CHRIST

Therefore we are buried with him by baptism into death: that like as Christ was raised up from the dead by the glory of the Father, even so we also should walk in newness of life. (Rom. 6:4)

For if we have been planted together in the likeness of his death, we shall be also in the likeness of his resurrection: (Rom 6:5)

Buried with him in baptism, wherein also ye are risen with him through the faith of the operation of God, who hath raised him from the dead. (Col. 2:12)

MADE ALIVE WITH CHRIST

Even when we were dead in sins, hath quickened us together with Christ, (by grace ye are saved;) (Eph 2:5)

And you, being dead in your sins and the uncircumcision of your flesh, hath he quickened together with him, having forgiven you all trespasses; (Col. 2:13)

RAISED WITH CHRIST

And hath raised us up together, and made us sit together in heavenly places in Christ Jesus: (Eph. 2:6)

> Buried with him in baptism, wherein also ye are risen with him through the faith of the operation of God, who hath raised him from the dead. (Col. 2:12)

> If ye then be risen with Christ, seek those things which are above, where Christ sitteth on the right hand of God. (Col. 3:1)

SEATED WITH CHRIST

> And what is the exceeding greatness of his power to us-ward who believe, according to the working of his mighty power, Which he wrought in Christ, when he raised him from the dead, and set him at his own right hand in the heavenly places,...And you...(Eph 1:19, 20; 2:1a)

> And hath raised us up together, and made us sit together in heavenly places in Christ Jesus: (Eph. 2:6)

Our spiritual union with Christ and participation with him in every step of his redemptive work is the mystery behind Jesus' statement that we must be born again. Our spirits are re-created and reborn through the process of being made alive with Christ in his resurrection. We are not just covered with a robe of righteousness or merely considered to be righteous. We have been re-created with a righteous new nature and reborn into a new spiritual realm and relationship with God.

Therefore if any man be in Christ, he is a new creature: old things are passed away; behold, all things
are become new. (2 Cor. 5:17)

For in Christ Jesus neither circumcision availeth
any thing, nor uncircumcision, but a new creature.
(Gal. 6:15)

For we are his workmanship, created in Christ
Jesus... (Eph. 2:10a)

And that ye put on the new man, which after God
is created in righteousness and true holiness. (Eph.
4:24)

Knowing that you have that kind of righteousness, that
you are accepted and approved by God and his favor is
upon you the same as it is upon Jesus, will affect your life
in ways that are beyond comprehension.

What does all this have to do with tithing? The righteous, new-creation man in Christ is a different kind of
person than ever existed before the resurrection. He lives in
a new spiritual realm with a different relationship to God
than anyone had before. He walks with God from the new
perspective of spiritual union with Christ. The finished
work of Christ is the foundation for everything he thinks
and does. He lives and moves and has his being in Christ.
He relates to everything from the position of being seated
with Christ at God's right hand. No other person in the
Bible is an accurate example of how the new-creation man
in Christ should live and walk with God. The only true

example is the resurrected Lord Jesus Christ and tithing is not part of his life, enthroned on high.

SALVATION IS MORE THAN FORGIVENESS

Salvation has not been understood for what it really is. That's why Christians think God's blessing and provision depend on tithing. They think salvation only includes our forgiveness and eternal destiny in heaven—that God's blessing, grace, and provision, for this present life, are based on things we do. That misunderstanding comes from an Old Covenant mentality. It isn't consistent with our new life in Christ and our relationship to God as sons.

Salvation is everything that God accomplished for our benefit on the cross. It includes everything we will ever receive from God, both now and in eternity. There is no blessing, grace, or provision that wasn't totally paid for at the cross. God has already given it all to us in Christ and we receive it all by faith.

God's work of salvation did not originate in the rational mind of man. No human mind could ever conceive something so wonderful. No reasonable person would dare ask God for the kind of grace that he extended to us through Christ. He gave us everything there was to give and there is nothing left to gain by tithing.

All of God's provision for this life as well as the life to come is only offered on his terms: pure grace through faith. He doesn't give us the option of creating our own hybrid doctrines of grace and works. He won't accommodate our religious systems, even if they are based on the story of someone in the Bible. We are now in the New Covenant and God has no pleasure in doctrines that seek to add to the finished work of Christ. He is pleased by faith that accepts his gift of righteousness and ceases from all personal efforts to achieve it.

The doctrine of tithing dilutes the message of perfect righteousness and complete salvation by free grace alone. It diminishes the goodness of God that has abundantly provided everything we need as a totally free gift with no requirement except faith. God has elevated our relationship with him to a place of honor such that we can now have the joy of living and doing everything from pure motives of love and gratitude, untainted by obligation, self-interest, or fear.

The doctrine of tithing also opens the door to our unseen spiritual enemy, Satan, who constantly seeks for an opportunity to work against us. Any church doctrine that diminishes the finished work of Christ on the cross, in any way, will be exploited by the devil to his greatest possible advantage. God's grace comes through faith. Putting just a little attention on our works is enough to stop it. That is why it only takes one wrong doctrine to nullify the power of Christ's resurrection. Galatians 5:9 says, "A little leaven leaveneth the whole lump."

GRACE AND WORKS DON'T MIX

The Bible is emphatic that righteousness by grace cannot be mixed with righteousness by works. They are mutually exclusive. Each one must be all-or-nothing.

> And if by grace, then is it no more of works: other-
> wise grace is no more grace. But if it be of works,
> then is it no more grace: otherwise work is no more
> work. (Rom. 11:6)

In Romans 4 Paul makes it clear that Abraham's righteousness and his receiving of God's promise were based on
faith and were a demonstration of God's pure grace, without any works on Abraham's part whatsoever. God's blessing on Abraham had nothing to do with tithing.

> For if Abraham were justified by works, he hath
> whereof to glory; but not before God. For what
> saith the scripture? Abraham believed God, and it
> was counted unto him for righteousness. Now to
> him that worketh is the reward not reckoned of
> grace, but of debt. But to him that worketh not, but
> believeth on him that justifieth the ungodly, his
> faith is counted for righteousness. (Rom. 4:2–5)

All of God's promises to us today are obtained by faith
through grace.

> Therefore it is of faith, that it might be by grace; to
> the end the promise might be sure to all the seed;
> not to that only which is of the law, but to that also
> which is of the faith of Abraham; who is the father
> of us all. (Rom. 4:16)

The book of Romans belabors the point that we are now
righteous, that it is all through the work of Christ on the
cross, and that it is a free gift. It leaves no room for the idea
that tithing could be a requirement for receiving anything

that God has provided through Jesus Christ. Romans 8:32 emphasizes the point that everything we receive from God is a free gift:

> He that spared not his own Son, but delivered him
> up for us all, how shall he not with him also freely
> give us all things?

Not only did God give his own son for us, he freely gave us every other thing that he had to give. He wasn't looking for anything from us but faith. God delights in faith. Faith pleases him in a way the natural mind cannot comprehend.

> Now the just shall live by faith: but if any man
> draw back, my soul shall have no pleasure in him.
> (Heb. 10:38)

Faith is the key to everything we receive from God. And since everything we receive from him is by grace, it is no surprise that even our faith is a gift to us from God.

> For by grace are ye saved through faith; and that
> not of yourselves: it is the gift of God: (Eph. 2:8)

The doctrine of tithing cannot be held by people without affecting their whole understanding of life in Christ. It colors their view of every individual subject, such as righteousness, grace, salvation, and blessing. It distorts the message of the finished work of Christ. It neutralizes the power of the New Covenant. It detracts from the glory of being a son of God in Christ, seated with him at the Father's right hand, and reigning in life. It diminishes God's goodness, it is a hindrance to his working, and it is inferior to the relationship that he expects to have with his sons.

The Father has given everything to the Son, Jesus, withholding nothing. The entire universe, every natural and spiritual dimension, now belongs to Christ and together with him we were made joint heirs of it all. There is nothing left to gain by tithing. All that remains for us is to lay aside the old low-realm mentalities of life and to grow up into full stature in Christ and begin to live like mature sons of God.

11

SONS OF GOD

IF you have been joined to Jesus Christ through faith, being born again by the power of the Holy Spirit, then you are a son of God. That is your reality and defining conscious identity. You are not waiting to become a son of God when you go to heaven; you are a son of God now.

Beloved, now are we the sons of God, (1 John 3:2a)

And because ye are sons, God hath sent forth the Spirit of his Son into your hearts, crying, Abba, Father. (Gal. 4:6)

That ye may be blameless and harmless, the sons of God, without rebuke, in the midst of a crooked and perverse nation, among whom ye shine as lights in the world; (Phil. 2:15)

Being a son of God is more than a figure of speech or a religious doctrine. Through union with Christ you have been spiritually reborn and re-created. You have been elevated to a place of actual sonship in God's family, sharing Jesus' life, inheritance, and standing with the Father. Knowing that fact is an absolute necessity for understanding the New Covenant and life in Christ.

> God is faithful, by whom ye were called unto the fellowship of his Son Jesus Christ our Lord. (1 Cor. 1:9)

> Faithful is God through whom you were divinely summoned into a joint-participation with His Son, Jesus Christ our Lord. (1 Cor. 1:9, Wuest)[1]

> Behold, what manner of love the Father hath bestowed upon us, that we should be called the sons of God: therefore the world knoweth us not, because it knew him not. (1 John 3:1)

Jesus Christ is God's only definition of a son. He was the pattern for all the sons that God would ever receive through him. As a son of God in Christ, you become the kind of son that Jesus is. You come to the Father through Jesus and enter the relationship through spiritual union. Jesus' finished work on the cross is accounted to you and you are born again in him. His spiritual life and identity becomes yours. Jesus' relationship to the Father becomes your relationship. You are to live and walk with the Father as Jesus does.

The Father's objective is to bring many sons into maturity and his standard for that is the full stature of the resurrected Lord Jesus Christ.

> For whom he did foreknow, he also did predestinate to be conformed to the image of his Son, that he might be the firstborn among many brethren. (Rom. 8:29)

> Till we all come in the unity of the faith, and of the knowledge of the Son of God, unto a perfect man, unto the measure of the stature of the fulness of Christ: (Eph. 4:13)

> For the earnest expectation of the creature waiteth for the manifestation of the sons of God. (Rom 8:19)

> For it became him, for whom are all things, and by whom are all things, in bringing many sons unto glory, to make the captain of their salvation perfect through sufferings. (Heb. 2:10)

New wine cannot be contained in old wineskins. Your new relationship with God, as a son through Jesus Christ, cannot be expressed through the former ways of living that were known before the resurrection. Life in Christ does not work by following the ways of men who were not born again. It was designed to be lived from the perspective of the resurrected Christ: being a son of God, seated at the Father's right hand, perfected in righteousness, living by an inner nature instead of external regulations. This is the key to entering the glorious destiny promised by God.

Sons of God live by the life and power of Christ who is in them, not by a religious system of rewards and punishments that are designed to control their behavior. The Law was a system of rewards and punishments. It was an external constraint. It does not pertain to sons.

> For as many as are led by the Spirit of God, they are the sons of God. (Rom. 8:14)

Sons of God support the work of God on earth without the threat of curses or the enticement of blessings. They do God's will because it is their nature. They live like Jesus would live on the earth because he is living in them.

> I am crucified with Christ: nevertheless I live; yet not I, but Christ liveth in me: (Gal. 2:20a)

> For it is God which worketh in you both to will and to do of his good pleasure. (Phil. 2:13)

> Whereunto I also labour, striving according to his working, which worketh in me mightily. (Col 1:29)

Sons of God have the nature of their Father. They also share his objectives. They live to accomplish his desires, not something separate of their own. That is why they don't need laws, rules, and principles of giving. They don't need a standard of 10 percent because they have already committed 100 percent. They don't need to be coerced into putting God's purposes first in their life because they were reborn with his purposes in their heart. They aren't locked into a mindless routine like tithing because they have the

Spirit of God in them who is greater and wiser than any generic system of giving. Tithing and all of its associated rules are unnecessary and irrelevant.

Children and servants cannot live like sons and they will never know the power or glory of being a son. They have to be told what to do. They have to be regulated and monitored by others. They must have laws to direct them and punishments to reprove them. They must have rewards to motivate them. They haven't internalized the family objective so they have to be treated as hirelings. Children, especially, are self-seeking and self-serving. Their affection is on the things of earth and their personal benefit. The Father's will has not yet become their own.

Very few in the church have an understanding of being anything more than a child or a servant. Both perspectives are Old Covenant mentalities that became obsolete at the resurrection. The church has not comprehended the message that Jesus has given to us through Paul the apostle. So the church continues to pattern itself after Old Testament examples of faith. Most teaching on giving appeals to Christians as children or servants and continues to hold them in a low spiritual realm.

Sons of God are empowered to prosper financially by the grace of God which is upon them through their union with Christ. As they follow the Holy Spirit and do the will of God they will prosper. They are empowered to succeed in every area of life by Christ who lives within them. But they must be taught the truth in order to live as God designed them to.

Sons of God have the same relationship to the Father that Jesus has. Since tithing is not part of Jesus' relationship, now that he has been resurrected, it is not part of their relationship. Since they are one with Jesus, they don't tithe to him either. They are joint owners of all things together with Christ by their spiritual union. Tithing was ordained for a different kind of relationship with God—not for sons.

> Wherefore thou art no more a servant, but a son; and if a son, then an heir of God through Christ. (Gal. 4:7)

> And if children, then heirs; heirs of God, and joint-heirs with Christ; (Rom 8:17a)

SOURCE OF SPIRITUAL LIFE

The source of life and motivation for the Christian is Christ who is living within him.

> I am crucified with Christ: nevertheless I live; yet not I, but Christ liveth in me: (Gal 2:20a)

> For it is God which worketh in you both to will and to do of his good pleasure. (Phil. 2:13)

Proverbs 6:6–7 says that the ant has no guide, overseer, or ruler yet prepares food in summer and gathers food in harvest. The ant has a God-given inner nature to direct its life. How much more should a God-indwelt Christian, who has been reborn with God's own divine nature, be able to be led by the Holy Spirit in their giving instead of needing to follow laws and external commandments like tithing.

GROWING UP SPIRITUALLY

Children need a law. That is what Galatians 4:1–3 says:

> Now I say, That the heir, as long as he is a child, dif-
> fereth nothing from a servant, though he be lord of
> all; But is under tutors and governors until the time
> appointed of the father. Even so we, when we were
> children, were in bondage under the elements of
> the world:

But the message of Galatians 4:4–5 is that in Christ we
are no longer children, we are mature sons:

> But when the fulness of the time was come, God
> sent forth his Son, made of a woman, made under
> the law, To redeem them that were under the law,
> that we might receive the adoption of sons.

Christians will be immature as long as they are kept
under laws. Following laws will keep them from learning
how to follow the leading of the Holy Spirit. In order for
them to grow up, someone must take away the carnal
things they rely on to direct their lives.

Many years ago I heard a story about a group of children on a playground next to a busy street. As long as a
fence was up they felt free to run and play anywhere.
When the fence was taken down they huddled together
near the building out of fear. Preachers have often used
such stories to make analogies that promote the necessity
of religious laws in our lives. If you think Christians must
always be spiritually immature then that conclusion would

be correct. However, adults would not react that way and that is the message in Galatians 3 and 4.

God created you to be a glorious demonstration of his life and nature to the world. You are a son of God like Jesus. You are a unique and vibrant new creation in him. You weren't designed live like a dumb sheep who can do nothing but follow laws and obey orders from other people. You have a direct and personal relationship to God. You have a new nature that can be led by the Holy Spirit to accomplish God's purposes without regard to tithing.

The doctrine of tithing distracts people from the real nature of our relationship with God: organic spiritual union and one-hundred-percent commitment. It also disconnects them from the realm of being led and empowered by the Holy Spirit. You cannot live from your new nature in Christ while you are trying to follow external regulations like tithing. The glorious life of Christ that you were created to enjoy comes from being an expression of Christ on earth not by following laws, rules, and principles.

Unshackle yourself from low-realm mentalities like tithing and begin to be who you are from the new nature of your inner man. Let Jesus Christ live through you. Possess the full benefit of Jesus' finished work on the cross and your position with him at the Father's right hand. Take his word and define your life by it. Let it establish your identity. Let it govern your self-image, your relationships, your plans, and your actions. Accept what God has done for you in Christ and enter into it. God planned it and performed it all for that purpose.

12

COMMENCEMENT

THIS book is about making a change from an obsolete and carnal way of living into a spiritual way of living in Christ, based on the New Covenant. It's about living like a person who is in union with Christ rather than a person who is separate from God. It's about entering a place of freedom in Christ to be led by the Spirit of God. Tithing is just one aspect of the old carnal way of thinking and relating to God, but it's a big hindrance that should be removed. The Holy Spirit is taking the church to a place of maturity in Christ and he has much further to go.

Some may still say, "I like to tithe, it works well for me, can't I do it if I want to?" Of course, you may give in whatever way you please. You have freedom in Christ. New Covenant giving is according to 2 Corinthians 9:7:

Every man according as he purposeth in his heart,
so let him give; not grudgingly, or of necessity: for
God loveth a cheerful giver.

However, God gave you that freedom so you could follow
the Holy Spirit and live by the divine nature of Christ that
came into you at the new birth. It would be a mistake to
waste that opportunity by continuing in the old carnal
ways of living, following the example of men who lived
before the resurrection, who couldn't be born again
through faith in Jesus Christ.

We have a relationship to God that beggars the imagina-
tion of previous generations. What God has done for man
through Christ was the crowning display of his wisdom
and power. His elevation of the new-creation man in union
with Christ, to a place at his right hand in the heavenlies,
surpasses all the hopes of the prophets who foretold of a
messiah to come. God's spiritual union with man and personal presence within, through the indwelling Holy Spirit,
has transformed the nature of his relationship with man. It
has redefined the meaning of a life that is pleasing to him.

We cannot base our present relationship with God on
the paradigms of the past. We will fall terribly short if we
do. Tithing was the best that could be done for the age it
was ordained. God was limited by the nature of the people
with whom he was working. They were not spiritually
reborn. They were not indwelt by the Holy Spirit to be led
and inspired individually. They had to be controlled and
directed externally. They had to be governed by a system of
laws and generic commandments.

Tithing was a crude system of stewardship: one law for everyone, everywhere, at all times. God was dealing with an unregenerate people on the level of their lowest common denominator. The Holy Spirit was not working directly and uniquely within each person in every situation. For the body of Christ to return to a spiritually primitive system of financial stewardship based on tithing would be like rejecting the knowledge of space travel to return to a world of ox carts.

THE SUPERIORITY OF JESUS

The Lord Jesus Christ now deals with each member of his body directly and individually through the infinite ability of the Holy Spirit. He strategically calls for contribution and participation according to his infinite knowledge and wisdom. No two people are identical and neither should be their giving. Their income, their assets, their abilities, their place in God's kingdom and their connection to his work are all different. Their giving should be just as unique. The days of laws and generic instructions are over.

God is too brilliant to be limited to a one-size-fits-all system of giving for the body of Christ. He is too creative to be satisfied with a kingdom of drones who walk in monotonous lockstep, mindlessly following an external requirement like tithing. No two plants, animals or even snowflakes are identical in God's creation. Why should we expect that two people will have the same expression of giving any more than we would expect them to have identical fingerprints? Why would giving be regimented under one undiscriminating law that takes no account of the uniqueness of every person and situation?

The Lord Jesus Christ owns all the resources in every believer's possession. He maintains his right to instant access, any time and any place in the world. His body was designed for peak performance when each member is responding to his specific direction. He moves his body and does his business at the speed of inspiration. He operates now in this higher dimension because of the Holy Spirit who is in every believer to instruct them directly.

Whether you tithe or not, the New Covenant presumes that you have a one-hundred-percent commitment to God. That means you live totally for him with everything you possess and you seek to follow the Holy Spirit's leading. So even if you tithe, God expects you to remember that the remaining 90 percent belongs to him just as much as the first 10 percent. And he expects that you will be just as attentive to his leading about how you should use it.

WHY WOULD YOU WANT TO TITHE?

If you still feel like you should tithe, you should ask yourself why. Do you think there is something spiritually better about tithing or being a tither? Do you think there is something special about 10 percent in the New Covenant? Are you still uncertain about being free from all preset percentages and practices of giving? Are you afraid that you will quit giving altogether if you don't regulate yourself with some kind of law? Do you feel nervous if you don't have some concrete way to judge how you are doing? Do you feel like you would be lost or disoriented without something external to guide you? Do you feel uncertain about having God's blessing, approval, and protection if you don't tithe?

All those questions relate to fundamental spiritual issues that are at the heart of the practice of tithing. Whether a person realizes it or not, their daily life is being governed and directed by the spiritual paradigm they have acquired. It influences everything in their relationship with God. It sets the limits of what he can do in and through them in this life. Continuing to follow a principle of tithing, when God has established a new and higher way of living, will tend to hold you in the all the other inferior ways of living that have now been superseded in Christ. It is not possible to enter the fullness of life in Christ as a son of God when you are still following ways of living that were ordained for people who were not born again.

The resurrected Lord Jesus Christ is the only objective standard for life as a son of God. Status quo Christianity does not portray who we are and what we have in Christ. The church is doing its best and the leaders should be appreciated, but we must not hesitate to question the doctrine that has been handed down to us. We must judge it in the light of God's word. We must follow the Holy Spirit as he leads the church to full stature in Christ.

SPIRITUALLY BETTER NOT TO TITHE

In answer to the question about continuing to tithe as a matter of freewill, you would be far better off to purge your

thinking of tithing and all of the other low-realm mentalities that are associated with it. Become single-minded in
your thinking about New Covenant life and your relationship to God as a son. Your spiritual life will be empowered
as your mind is renewed to the conscious reality of a son of
God. You will be transformed into a person who is guided
and motivated by the Holy Spirit. You will rise to the level
of power and authority that God has ordained for sons.

As long as your mind is open to the possibility that you
should tithe, it will also be opened to weakness, confusion,
error, and double-mindedness. The flesh has an unending
temptation to latch onto something it can do to gain more
favor or blessing from God. The carnal, religious mind
gravitates to laws, principles, and systems of behavior that
it can perform to maintain its control over the events of life.

NOTHING TO GAIN BY TITHING

All of God's righteousness, salvation, blessing, grace,
and approval come to us through the death, burial, and resurrection of Jesus. Tithing cannot and does not add one
single thing—it actually diminishes the finished work of
Christ. That is a hard thing for the carnal mind to accept
and it requires a constant commitment of faith to stay fixed
on that truth. As long as tithing is an option, the carnal religious mind will prefer it and take confidence in it.

You don't need to tithe to prosper spiritually. You don't
need to tithe to prosper financially. You don't need to tithe
to receive God's full, covenant provision for health and
strength. You don't need to tithe to have God's complete

blessing, favor, and protection upon you and your family. You don't need to tithe to open the windows of heaven. You are already seated with Christ at the Father's right hand in heavenly places.

> Even when we were dead in sins, hath quickened us together with Christ, (by grace ye are saved;)
>
> And hath raised us up together, and made us sit together in heavenly places in Christ Jesus: (Eph. 2:5–6)

You are already blessed with every blessing that heaven has to offer.

> Blessed be the God and Father of our Lord Jesus Christ, who hath blessed us with all spiritual blessings in heavenly places in Christ: (Eph. 1:3)

Quit trying to open the windows of heaven and get a blessing poured out. Quit seeking after something you already have. Believe that you are seated at the Father's right hand and that all things are yours in Christ. Live in the reality of the finished work of Christ and all that it includes. Faith is the key. Believe God's word and act on it in the wisdom of the Holy Spirit.

The Father hasn't withheld anything from the Son and we have joint ownership of it all through our union with him. That is the glory of the finished work of the cross. God has nothing left that he could give us in return for tithing and he isn't looking for anything but faith anyway. You don't need to tithe to have any part of God's total salvation.

Tithing is an expression of devotion to God by many sincere people. But that doesn't change the fact that it is part of a low-realm, obsolete, and defunct mentality that brings weakness and confusion into the minds of Christians. We are supposed to be living like sons of God on earth and reigning in life by Jesus Christ. The tithing mentality obscures the reality of our glorious relationship and standing with God as sons, enthroned with Christ at the Father's right hand.

Whatever confidence that Christians gain by tithing is an illusion. Whatever sense of benefit or advantage they feel is really the confidence of the flesh in performing a religious work. God, in his goodness, will often honor sincere mistakes. He responds to faith. He can bless people when they are doing something that requires them to trust him. Their testimony of blessing is no validation of their doctrine, it is proof of God's goodness and his high regard for faith. They may have some measure of blessing but not to the degree they would have if they knew the truth and would begin to live like sons of God in Christ.

God rewards almost any kind of faith he can find, even misdirected faith that is sincerely following Old Testament patterns of worship. The Bible is full of examples that show the overwhelming preeminence that God gives to faith. Man, in his natural carnal mentality, thinks that works and deeds are God's highest priority. The tithing doctrine fits well with that carnal perspective.

In the matter of knowing how much money to give to churches or ministries, the answer is simply to ask the Lord and do as he leads. It isn't hard or complicated. The born-again believer in Jesus Christ has been re-created by design to be led by the Holy Spirit; it is as natural to him as breathing. There is no reason to be afraid of making a mistake. God is pleased by faith and it is an act of faith to trust that you are now a son of God through Jesus Christ, that you are completely righteous by his shed blood, and that you are now led by the Holy Spirit.

FULL STATURE IN CHRIST

When your doctrine is cleansed of tithing and soundly based on the finished work of the cross, you will enter a whole new level of spiritual strength, authority, and boldness. You will experience a new dimension of love and gratitude toward God for all he has done for you in Christ. You will begin to taste the glorious freedom of real life in Christ. You will start to be fully alive in Christ as you were created to be. It will be the beginning of a lifelong journey toward full-statured maturity as a son of God in Christ.

The gospel is the message of the finished work of Christ and our sharing with him of his resurrected life. If we would preach that message we would see more faith, more commitment, and more action from Christians. We would also see more money given to support the work of God than the tithing message has ever produced.

By the grace of God, let's leave the obsolete mentalities and patterns of living that were given to men who lived before the resurrection. Let's enter the realm of true spiritual life in Christ and begin to express his life through us now. The glorious life that God intended is far better than the status quo of religion, but we have to turn loose of the old to enter into the new.

APPENDIX

HEBREWS 7

The book of Hebrews is comparing the Old Covenant and the New, demonstrating that we have a totally different and better relation to God than men under the Law of Moses. The discussion of tithing in Hebrews chapter 7 was only included to prove that the priesthood of Melchizedek was superior to the Levitical priesthood. By proving that point the writer would also prove that Jesus is superior to the priests of the Old Covenant because Psalm 110:4 had prophesied that he would be a priest forever, "after the order of Melchizedek." That was the ultimate purpose of the argument, to prove that Jesus was greater than the Old Covenant priests.

Tithing is part of the comparison and the argument because the tribe of Levi was symbolically in the loins of their great-grandfather Abraham when he met Melchizedek and gave him a tithe. Therefore it can be said that Levi paid a tithe to Melchizedek and received a blessing from him. Paying the tithe to Melchizedek and receiving the blessing from him are both considered by the writer of Hebrews to be proof that Melchizedek was greater than Levi and all the Old Covenant priests, which came from the tribe of Levi. (Heb. 7:1–17)

The priesthood of Melchizedek can also be considered greater than the Old Covenant priesthood because Melchizedek was a king and a priest and the Levitical priesthood was forbidden to hold the office of king.

Furthermore, under the Law of Moses there was a constant succession of priests as men would die and be replaced. The priesthood of Melchizedek can also be considered superior to this aspect of the Levitical priesthood due to the fact that there is no Biblical reference to his birth or death or being replaced by any other after him.

NOT TEACHING TITHING TO THE CHURCH

Hebrews 7:8 has been taken out of context and misinterpreted. It is erroneously considered by some to be teaching that tithing is the customary way of giving in the New Covenant. This passage of scripture is part of a weighty and complex theological argument. The casual reader may not comprehend its meaning. It requires a careful study of the whole passage, verse by verse and word by word, to get a clear understanding of what is being said.

Hebrews 7:8 in the King James Version reads:

> And here men that die receive tithes; but there he receiveth them, of whom it is witnessed that he liveth.

This verse is absolutely not saying that the practice of tithing was being followed by the New Testament church at the time the book of Hebrews was written. It is also not talking about a practice of tithing that is supposed to be in effect permanently, throughout the church age. The phrase "here men that die receive tithes" is not talking about Christian ministers in the church, now or then. It is talking about priests at the temple in Jerusalem. The "he" that is being referred to by the phrase "but there he receiveth them" is Melchizedek, 4000 years ago, not Jesus.

This verse is incorrectly interpreted by some to say in effect:

> And here (in the New Covenant), men that die (our pastors and other ministers) receive tithes (from born-again Christians); but there (up in heaven) he (Jesus) (is the one who actually) is receiving them, of whom it is witnessed that he liveth.

This erroneous interpretation of the verse does not comprehend the theological argument that is being made in the passage. This misinterpretation is carelessly taken to be a scriptural proof that tithing is the will of God and the standard mode of operation in the New Covenant.

Objectively interpreted within its context, the verse is actually saying:

> And here (in Israel at the time that Hebrews was written) men (who are priests under the Old Covenant) that (will eventually) die (and be succeeded by another mortal man after them) receive tithes (from those who are following the Law of Moses); but there (2000 years prior, during the time of Abraham in Genesis 14) he (Melchizedek) receiveth them, of whom it is witnessed that he liveth.

Scholars and theologians debate whether this language referring to Melchizedek's endless life is literal or symbolic.

In either case the verse is not a reference to tithing in the New Covenant. "Here men that die receive tithes" is referring to Old Covenant priests not to New Covenant ministers. "There he receiveth them" is referring to Melchizedek in Genesis 14:18–20, not to Jesus up in heaven now. Nowhere in the verse is the New Covenant being referred to. This passage is not teaching that tithing is the way of giving that God has ordained for the New Covenant.

Consider some other translations of Hebrews 7:8:

> Furthermore, here [in the Levitical priesthood] tithes are received by men who are subject to death; while there [in the case of Melchizedek], they are received by one of whom it is testified that he lives [perpetually]. (The Amplified Bible. Copyright © Zondervan Publishing House 1965)

> And here, on the one hand, men subject to death are receiving tithes, but there he [Melchisedec] receives them, concerning whom the testimony is that he is living. (The New Testament: An Expanded Translation by Kenneth S. Wuest. Copyright © Wm. B. Eerdmans Publishing Co. 1961)

The "he" referred to in Hebrews 7:8 is the same "he" referred to in verse 6. That "he" is Melchizedek. That "he" is not referring to Jesus in the New Covenant. Melchizedek is the subject of verse 1 and is referred to in verses 2, 3, 4, 6, 8, 10, 11, 15, 17, and 21.

Therefore the tithe mentioned in verse 8 is not a reference to tithing in the New Covenant. It is a reference to the tithe Abraham gave to Melchizedek. Even if Melchizedek was actually a pre-incarnate appearance of Jesus Christ, he was in a different relationship to Abraham than he is to the born-again man in the New Covenant. God's relationship with man changed drastically at the resurrection of Jesus. We don't relate to God like Abraham did.

HIGHER AND BETTER THAN ABRAHAM

We have a far higher and better relationship to Jesus Christ than Abraham had to Melchizedek. The dynamics of our relationship, through spiritual union with Christ, are completely different than those between Abraham and Melchizedek. We are sons of God through Christ, sharing his position, status, and relationship to the Father. Jesus isn't tithing to the Father so neither do we. We don't tithe to Jesus because we are one with him. That would be inconsistent with our relationship.

Everything in our possession is already jointly possessed by Jesus Christ because he is our life, living in us. Everything we have is presumed to be committed to his purposes. We are stewards who live to accomplish his will on earth. But tithing is not the pattern we follow today. The Holy Spirit is the leader now, not the principle of tithing.

Hebrews 7 is part of a theological argument that Jesus is a greater high priest than the high priest of the Old Covenant and that we are living in a completely different spiritual system in the New Covenant. Tithing was only included as part of the comparison between Melchizedek and the Old Covenant priests. Hebrews 7 is not a description of tithing or giving by Christians in the early days of the church. It cannot be used to support the statement that tithing was "after the Law." It is not an instruction to tithe. It is not a suggestion to tithe. It is not even a comment on tithing in the New Covenant.

How to Be Born Again

This book was written primarily to people who have a personal relationship with God through Jesus Christ, who is their Lord and Savior. If you do not, the following information will tell you how you may come to know him and be certain about your eternal salvation.

Salvation was very costly and difficult for God to accomplish but he has made it very simple and easy for us to receive. It is a free gift that we receive by faith. God has offered it to anyone who will accept it.

Jesus died on the cross for our sin, he was buried, and he rose again on the third day. His shed blood paid the price for our complete forgiveness and salvation. He ascended up into heaven and is seated at the Father's right hand, where he lives to be our Savior.

If you would like to be spiritually reborn and enter a personal relationship with God, with him as your father and you as his child, you can do that right now. If you are not sure if you have a relationship with God and would like to be certain, you can settle that question in your heart.

Just believe and make a decision of your will. The expression of your heart is the issue, not the specific words that you pray. But here is an example that you may follow if you would like to have an idea of what to say:

> Dear Lord Jesus, I believe that you died on the cross for my sin, that you were buried, that you

rose again on the third day, and that you are now seated at the Father's right hand in heaven. I accept your free gift of salvation and I give myself to you. Please come into my heart and be my Lord and Savior. I receive you now. Thank you. I believe that I am now born again and saved to live with you in heaven forever. Please teach me how to live in the new relationship that I now have with you and the Heavenly Father and the Holy Spirit. Amen.

If you have just accepted the Lord Jesus Christ into your heart and life we would love to hear about it. Please send us a letter or an e-mail.

Tekoa Publishing
P.O. Box 977
Graham, NC 27253

E-mail address: mail@tekoapublishing.com

If you would like more information about your new relationship with God and how to learn to live as a child of God in this life please visit our web site.

Web address: www.tekoapublishing.com

NOTES

Chapter 5 – AFTER THE LAW

1. Acts 20:28; 1 Cor. 6:19, 20; Eph. 1:7; Col. 1:14; Heb. 9:12; 1 Pet. 1:18–19; Rev. 1:5, 5:9.

2. Matt. 26:28; Acts 10:43; Eph. 1:7; Col. 1:14; Heb. 9:11–14, 10:1–23.

3. 1 Cor. 12:13; Gal. 3:27.

4. John 14:16, 17, 20, 23, 17:21, 23; 1 Cor. 6:17; Eph. 5:30, 32.

5. Rom. 6:2–11; Gal. 2:20, 6:14; Col. 3:3.

6. John 3:3–8; 1 Cor. 6:9–11; 2 Cor. 5:17, 18, 21; Gal. 6:15; Eph. 2:10, 4:24; Col. 3:9, 10; Titus 3:5; 1 Pet. 1:3, 23; 2 Pet. 1:4; 1 John 4:17.

7. John 1:12; Rom. 8:14, 19, 29; Gal. 4:6, 7; Eph. 2:5, 6; Heb 2:10, 11, 12:7; 1 John 3:1, 2.

8. Rom. 5:19; 1 Cor. 1:30, 6:11; 2 Cor. 5:21, 6:14; Eph. 4:24.

9. John 15:4, 5, 17:21–23; Rom. 8:10; 2 Cor. 13:5; Gal. 2:20; Eph. 3:17; Col 1:27, 3:11; 1 John 3:23, 24, 4:4.

10. 1 Cor. 3:16, 6:19; 2 Cor. 6:16.

11. John 7:39, 14:16, 17, 16:7–15; Acts 2:4; Rom. 8:9, 11, 14, 15, 23, 26; 1 Cor. 2:12; 2 Cor. 5:5; Gal 3:2, 14, 4:6, 5:18; Eph. 3:16; 1 Thess. 4:8; 1 John 3:24, 4:13.

12. Luke 1:68–74; John 5:24; Rom. 5:17, 6:6, 7, 12, 14, 18, 22, 8:2; Gal 3:13; Col. 1:13, 2:15; Heb. 2:14, 15.

13. Eph. 1:19–2:1, 2:4–6; Col. 2:12, 13, 3:1.

14. Eph. 1:3; Rom. 8:32; 1 Cor. 3:21, 22; 2 Pet. 1:3.

15. Rom. 4:13, 8:17; 1 Cor. 3:21, 22; Gal 3:7, 14, 16, 29, 4:7;
     Heb. 1:2.

16. Matt. 28:18–20; Mark 16:15–20; Luke 10:19; John
     14:13, 14, 15:16, 16:23, 24, 26; 2 Cor. 10:3–5; Eph. 1:
     19–23, 2:6; Phil. 2:9–11; Col. 2:9, 10; Heb. 10:12–14.

17. John 14:12; Rom. 5:17; Eph. 4:13–15; 1 John 2:6, 4:17.

Chapter 9 – DISINFORMATION III

1. "Americans Were More Generous in 2001 Than in
    2000." Barna Research Online. 9 Apr. 2002. Barna
    Research Group of Ventura, California. 1 June 2002
    <http://www.barna.org/cgi-bin/PagePressRelease
    .asp?PressReleaseID=110&Reference=F>.

Chapter 11 – Sons of God

1. The New Testament: An Expanded Translation by
    Kenneth S. Wuest. Copyright (c) Wm. B. Eerdmans
    Publishing Co. 1961.

INDEX OF
DISINFORMATION TOPICS

MESSAGE FROM TEKOA PUBLISHING

Tekoa Publishing proclaims the message of life in Christ as a son of God, in this present world, as well as a future of living and reigning with Christ eternally, throughout the ages to come. The truth of God's word will make you strong. It will make you free. It will bring you to the full measure of the stature of Christ. That is God's destiny for every person who comes to him through faith in Jesus Christ.

If you have been blessed by this book we would like to hear about it. If you would like more information about living as a son of God in Christ—knowing God, fulfilling your call, possessing your inheritance and reigning in life—please visit our web site.

Tekoa Publishing
P.O. Box 977
Graham, NC 27253

Web address: www.tekoapublishing.com

E-mail address: mail@tekoapublishing.com

Personal Notes